Personal Health
Self-Assessments and
Health Almanac for

An Invitation to Health
Brief Fourth Edition

Dianne Hales

THOMSON

WADSWORTH

Australia • Canada • Mexico • Singapore • Spain • United Kingdom • United States

Personal Health Self-Assessments and Health Almanac for
An Invitation to Health
Brief Fourth Edition
Dianne Hales

Executive Editor: *Nedah Rose*
Assistant Editor: *Seth Dobrin*
Editorial Assistant: *Colin Blake*
Marketing Manager: *Jennifer Somerville*
Project Manager, Editorial Production: *Sandra Craig*
Print Buyer: *Judy Inouye*

Permissions Editor: *Sarah Harkrader*
Production: *The Book Company*
Cover Designer: *Norman Baugher*
Cover Image: *Nathan Bilow/Getty Images*
Compositor: *Parkwood Composition Service*
Printer: *Quebecor World/Dubuque*

For more information about our products, contact us at:
Thomson Learning Academic Resource Center
1-800-423-0563
For permission to use material from this text or product, submit a request online at
http://www.thomsonrights.com
Any additional questions about permissions can be submitted by email to **thomsonrights@thomson.com**.

ISBN 0-495-01488-5

Thomson Higher Education
10 Davis Drive
Belmont, CA 94002-3098
USA

Asia (including India)
Thomson Learning
5 Shenton Way
#01-01 UIC Building
Singapore 068808

Australia/New Zealand
Thomson Learning Australia
102 Dodds Street
Southbank, Victoria 3006
Australia

Canada
Thomson Nelson
1120 Birchmount Road
Toronto, Ontario M1K 5G4
Canada

UK/Europe/Middle East/Africa
Thomson Learning
High Holborn House
50–51 Bedford Row
London WC1R 4LR
United Kingdom

Latin America
Thomson Learning
Seneca, 53
Colonia Polanco
11560 Mexico
D.F. Mexico

Spain (including Portugal)
Thomson Paraninfo
Calle Magallanes, 25
28015 Madrid, Spain

Contents

What Is Wellness?*
by John W. Travis, M.D.

Most of us think in terms of illness, and assume that the absence of illness indicates wellness. There are actually many degrees of wellness, just as there are many degrees of illness. The Wellness Inventory is designed to stir up your thinking about many areas of wellness.

While people often lack physical symptoms, they may still be bored, depressed, tense, anxious, or generally unhappy with their lives. Such emotional states often set the stage for physical and mental disease. Even cancer may be brought on through the lowering of the body's resistance from excessive stress. These same emotional states can also lead to abuse of the body through smoking, over-drinking, and overeating. Such behaviors are usually substitutes for other, more basic human needs such as recognition from others, a more stimulating environment, caring and affection from friends, and greater self-acceptance.

Wellness is not a static state. High-level wellness involves giving good care to your physical self, using your mind constructively, expressing your emotions effectively, being creatively involved with those around you, and being concerned about your physical, psychological and spiritual environments.

Instructions:

Set aside a half hour for yourself in a quiet place where you will not be disturbed while taking the Inventory. Record your responses to each statement in the columns to the right where:

2 = Yes, usually
1 = Sometimes, maybe
0 = No, rarely

Select the answer that best indicates how true the statement is for you presently.

After you have responded to all the appropriate statements in each section, compute your average score for that section and transfer it to the corresponding box provided around the Wellness Inventory Wheel on page 3. Your completed Wheel will give you a clear presentation of the balance you have given to the many dimensions of your life.

You will find some of the statements are really two in one. We do this to show an important relationship between the two parts—usually an awareness of an issue, combined with an action based on that awareness. Mentally average your score for the two parts of the question.

---

*Abridged from the Wellness Index in *The Wellness Workbook*, Travis & Ryan, Ten Speed Press, 1988. Used with the permission of John Travis, M.D. www.thewellspring.com.

Each statement describes what we believe to be a wellness attribute. Because much wellness information is subjective and "unprovable" by current scientific methods, you (and possibly other authorities as well), may not agree with our conclusions. Many of the statements have further explanation in a footnote (noted with an asterisk). We ask only that you keep an open mind until you have studied available information, then decide.

This questionnaire was designed to educate more than to test. All statements are worded so that you can easily tell what we think are wellness attributes (which also makes it easy to "cheat" on your score). This means there can be no trick questions to test your honesty or consistency—the higher your score, the greater you believe your wellness to be. Full responsibility is placed on you to answer each statement as honestly as possible. It's not your score but what you learn about yourself that is most important.

If you decide that a statement does not apply to you, or you don't want to answer it, you can skip it and not be penalized in your score.

Transfer your average score from each section to the corresponding box around the Wheel. Then graph your score by drawing a curved line between the "spokes" that define each segment. (Use the scale provided—beginning at the center with 0.0 and reaching 2.0 at the circumference.) Last, fill in the corresponding amount of each wedge-shaped segment, using different colors if possible.

Your Health Change Plan: How to Make a Change

When you have completed the Wellness Inventory, study your wheel's shape and balance. How smoothly would it roll? What does it tell you? Are there any surprises in it? How does it feel to you? What don't you like about it? What do you like about it?

We recommend that you use colored pens to go back over the questions, noting the ones on which your scores were low and choosing some areas on which you are interested in working. It is easy to overwhelm yourself by taking on too many areas at once. Ignore, for now, those of lower priority to you. Remember, if you don't enjoy at least some aspects of the changes you are making, they probably won't last.

Here are some guidelines to help you as you change

:: Get support from friends, but don't expect them to supply all the reinforcement you need. You may join a group of overweight individuals and rely on their encouragement to stick to your diet. That's a great way to get going; but in the long run, your own commitment to losing weight has got to be strong enough to help you keep eating right and light.

:: Focus on the immediate rewards of your new behavior. You may stop smoking so that you'll live longer, but take note of every other benefit it brings you—more stamina, less coughing, more spending money, no more stale tobacco taste in your mouth.

:: Remind yourself of past successes you've had in making changes. Give yourself pep talks, commending yourself on how well you've done so far and how well you'll continue to do. This will boost your self-confidence.

:: Reward yourself regularly. Plan a pleasant reward as an incentive for every week you stick to your new behavior—sleeping in on a Saturday morning, going out with some friends, or spending a sunny afternoon outdoors. Small, regular rewards are more effective in keeping up motivation than one big reward that won't come for many months.

:: Expect and accept some relapses. The greatest rate of relapse occurs in the first few weeks after making a behavior change. During this critical time, get as much support as you can. In addition, work hard on self-motivation, reminding yourself daily of what you have to gain by sticking with your new health habit.

	Yes, usually	Sometimes, maybe	No, rarely
	2	1	0

1. I am an adventurous thinker. — ✔
2. I have no expectations, yet look to the future optimistically. — ✔ (Sometimes, maybe)
3. I am a nonsmoker. — ✔
4. I love long, hot baths. — ✔ (No, rarely)

Total points for this section = **5**   **4** + **1** + **0**

Divided by **4** (number of statements answered) = **1.3** Average score for this section.

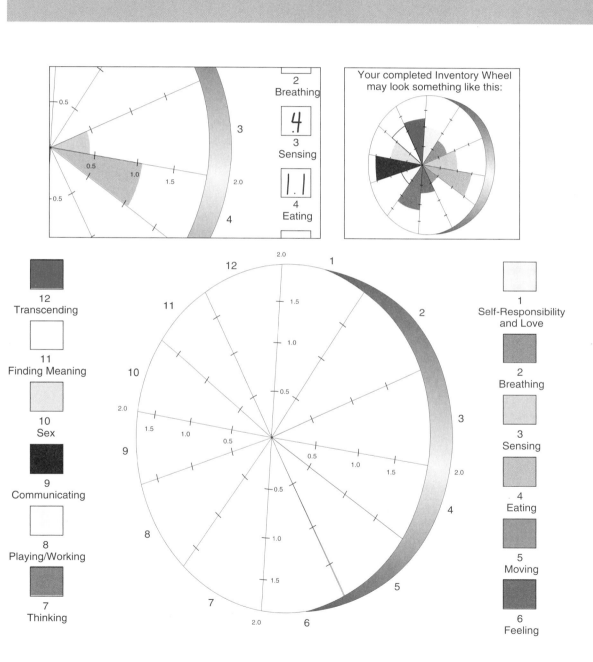

Your completed Inventory Wheel may look something like this:

2 Breathing
3 Sensing

.4
3 Sensing

1.1
4 Eating

12 Transcending
11 Finding Meaning
10 Sex
9 Communicating
8 Playing/Working
7 Thinking

1 Self-Responsibility and Love
2 Breathing
3 Sensing
4 Eating
5 Moving
6 Feeling

Section 1 — Wellness, Self-Responsibility and Love

	Yes, usually	Sometimes, maybe	No, rarely
	2	1	0
1. I believe how I live my life is an important factor in determining my state of health, and I live it in a manner consistent with that belief.	___	___	___
2. I vote regularly.[1]	___	___	___
3. I feel financially secure.	___	___	___
4. I conserve materials/energy at home and at work.[2]	___	___	___
5. I protect my living area from fire and safety hazards.	___	___	___
6. I use dental floss and a soft toothbrush daily.	___	___	___
7. I am a nonsmoker.	___	___	___
8. I am always sober when driving or operating dangerous machinery.	___	___	___
9. I wear a safety belt when I ride in a vehicle.	___	___	___
10. I understand the difference between blaming myself for a problem and simply taking responsibility (ability to respond) for that problem.	___	___	___

Total points for this section = ☐   ___ + ___ + ___

Divided by ___ (number of statements answered) = ___ Average score for this section.
(Transfer to the Wellness Inventory Wheel on **p. 3**)

Section 2 — Wellness and Breathing

	Yes, usually	Sometimes, maybe	No, rarely
	2	1	0
1. I stop during the day to become aware of the way I am breathing.	___	___	___
2. I meditate or relax myself for at least 15 to 20 minutes each day.	___	___	___
3. I can easily touch my hands to my toes when standing with knees straight.[3]	___	___	___
4. In temperatures over 70° F (21° C), my fingers feel warm when I touch my lips.[4]	___	___	___
5. My nails are healthy and I do not bite or pick at them.	___	___	___
6. I enjoy my work and do not find it overly stressful.	___	___	___
7. My personal relationships are satisfying.	___	___	___
8. I take time out for deep breathing several times a day.	___	___	___
9. I have plenty of energy.	___	___	___
10. I am at peace with myself.	___	___	___

Total points for this section = ☐   ___ + ___ + ___

Divided by ___ (number of statements answered) = ___ Average score for this section.
(Transfer to the Wellness Inventory Wheel on **p. 3**)

---

[1] Voting is a simple measure of your willingness to participate in the social system, which ultimately impacts your state of health.

[2] Besides recycling glass, paper, aluminum, and other recyclables, if you purchase products that are reusable rather than disposable, and are packaged with a minimum of material, you will reduce the drain of resources and the toxic load on the environment caused by the disposal of wastes.

[3] A lack of spinal flexibility is usually a symptom of chronic muscle tension as well as indicative of a poor balance of physical activities.

[4] If your hand temperature is below 85° F (30° C) in a warm room, you're cutting off circulation to your hands via an overactive sympathetic nervous system. You can learn to warm your hands with biofeedback and to thereby better relax.

Section 3 Wellness and Sensing

	Yes, usually	Sometimes, maybe	No, rarely
	2	1	0
1. My place of work has mostly natural lighting or full-spectrum fluorescent lighting.[5]	___	___	___
2. I avoid extremely noisy areas or wear protective ear covers.[6]	___	___	___
3. I take long walks, hikes, or other outings to actively explore my surroundings.	___	___	___
4. I give myself presents, treats, or nurture myself in other ways.	___	___	___
5. I enjoy getting, and can acknowledge, compliments and recognition from others.	___	___	___
6. It is easy for me to give sincere compliments and recognition to other people.	___	___	___
7. At times I like to be alone.	___	___	___
8. I enjoy touching or hugging other people.[7]	___	___	___
9. I enjoy being touched or hugged by others.[8]	___	___	___
10. I get and enjoy backrubs or massages.	___	___	___

Total points for this section = ☐   ___ + ___ + ___

Divided by _____ (number of statements answered) = _____ Average score for this section.
(Transfer to the Wellness Inventory Wheel on **p. 3**)

Section 4 Wellness and Eating

	Yes, usually	Sometimes, maybe	No, rarely
	2	1	0
1. I am aware of the difference between refined carbohydrates and complex carbohydrates and eat a majority of the latter.[9]	___	___	___
2. I think my diet is well balanced and wholesome.	___	___	___
3. I drink fewer than five alcoholic drinks per week.	___	___	___
4. I drink fewer than two cups of coffee or black (nonherbal) tea per day.[10]	___	___	___
5. I drink fewer than five soft drinks per week.[11]	___	___	___
6. I add little or no salt to my food.[12]	___	___	___
7. I read the labels for the ingredients of all processed foods I buy and I inquire as to the level of toxic chemicals used in production of fresh foods—choosing the purest available to me.	___	___	___
8. I eat at least two raw fruits or vegetables each day.	___	___	___
9. I have a good appetite and am within 15% of my ideal weight.	___	___	___
10. I can tell the difference between "stomach hunger" and "mouth hunger," and I don't stuff myself when I am experiencing only "mouth hunger."[13]	___	___	___

Total points for this section = ☐   ___ + ___ + ___

Divided by _____ (number of statements answered) = _____ Average score for this section.
(Transfer to the Wellness Inventory Wheel on **p. 3**)

[5] Full-spectrum light, like sunlight, contains many different wavelengths. Most eyeglasses, and the glass windows in your home or car, block the "near" ultraviolet light needed by your body. Special bulbs and lenses are available.

[6] Loud noises that leave your ears ringing cause irreversible and cumulative nerve damage over time. Ear plugs/muffs, obtained in sporting goods stores, should be worn around power saws, heavy equipment, and rock concerts!

[7,8] Long recognized by hospitals as therapeutic, touch can be a powerful preventative as well.

[9] Refined carbohydrates (white flour, sugar, white rice, alcohol, and others) are burned up by the body very quickly and contain no minerals or vitamins. Complex carbohydrates (fruits and vegetables) burn evenly and provide the bulk of dietary nutrients.

[10] Coffee and nonherbal teas contain stimulants that, when overused, abuse your body's adrenal glands.

[11] Besides caffeine, the empty calories in these chemical brews may cause a sugar "crash" shortly after drinking. Artificially sweetened ones may be worse. Consider the other nutrients you won't be getting, and the prices!

[12] In addition to having a presumed connection with high blood pressure, the salting of foods during cooking draws out minerals, which are lost when the water is poured off.

[13] Stomach hunger is a signal that your body needs food. Mouth hunger is a signal that it needs something else (attention/acknowledgement), which you are not getting, so it asks for food, a readily available "substitute."

Section 5 — Wellness and Moving

	Yes, usually	Sometimes, maybe	No, rarely
	2	1	0
1. I climb stairs rather than ride elevators.[14]	____	____	____
2. My daily activities include moderate physical effort.[15]	____	____	____
3. My daily activities include vigorous physical effort.[16]	____	____	____
4. I run at least 1 mile three times a week (or equivalent aerobic exercise).[17]	____	____	____
5. I run at least 3 miles three times a week (or equivalent aerobic exercise).	____	____	____
6. I do some form of stretching/limbering exercise for 10 to 20 minutes at least three times per week.[18]	____	____	____
7. I do some form of stretching/limbering exercise for 10 to 20 minutes at least six times per week.	____	____	____
8. I enjoy exploring new and effective ways of caring for myself through the movement of my body.	____	____	____
9. I enjoy stretching, moving, and exerting my body.	____	____	____
10. I am aware of and respond to messages from my body about its needs for movement.	____	____	____

Total points for this section = ☐   ____ + ____ + ____

Divided by _____ (number of statements answered) = ____ Average score for this section.
(Transfer to the Wellness Inventory Wheel on **p. 3**)

Section 6 — Wellness and Feeling

	Yes, usually	Sometimes, maybe	No, rarely
	2	1	0
1. I am able to feel and express my anger in ways that solve problems, rather than swallow anger or store it up.[19]	____	____	____
2. I allow myself to experience a full range of emotions and find constructive ways to express them.	____	____	____
3. I am able to say "no" to people without feeling guilty.	____	____	____
4. I laugh often and easily.	____	____	____
5. I feel OK about crying and allow myself to do so when appropriate.[20]	____	____	____
6. I listen to and consider others' criticisms of me rather than react defensively.	____	____	____
7. I have at least five close friends.	____	____	____
8. I like myself and look forward to the rest of my life.	____	____	____
9. I easily express concern, love and warmth to those I care about.	____	____	____
10. I can ask for help when needed.	____	____	____

Total points for this section = ☐   ____ + ____ + ____

Divided by _____ (number of statements answered) = ____ Average score for this section.
(Transfer to the Wellness Inventory Wheel on **p. 3**)

---

[14] If a long elevator ride is necessary, try getting off five flights below your destination. Urge building managers to keep stair doors unlocked.

[15] Moderate = rearing young children, gardening, scrubbing floors, brisk walking, and so on.

[16] Vigorous = heavy construction work, farming, moving heavy objects by hand, and so on.

[17] An aerobic exercise (like running) should keep your heart rate at about 60% of its maximum (120–150 bpm) for 12–20 minutes. Brisk walking for 20 minutes every day can produce effects similar to aerobic exercise.

[18] The stretching of muscles is important for maintaining maximum flexibility of joints and ligaments. It feels good, too.

[19] Learning to take charge of your emotions and using them to solve problems can prevent disease, improve communications, and increase your self-awareness. Suppressing emotions or using them to manipulate others is destructive to all.

[20] Crying over a loss relieves the body of pent-up feelings. In our culture males often have a difficult time allowing themselves to cry, while females may have learned to cry when angry, using tears as a means of manipulation.

Section 7 — Wellness and Thinking

	Yes, usually	Sometimes, maybe	No, rarely
	2	1	0
1. I am in charge of the subject matter and the emotional content of my thoughts, and am satisfied with what I choose to think about.[21]	____	____	____
2. I am aware that I make judgments wherein I think I am "right" and others are "wrong."[22]	____	____	____
3. It is easy for me to concentrate.	____	____	____
4. I am conscious of changes (such as breathing pattern, muscle tension, skin moisture, and so on) in my body in response to certain thoughts.[23]	____	____	____
5. I notice my perceptions of the world are colored by my thoughts at the time.[24]	____	____	____
6. I am aware that my thoughts are influenced by my environment.	____	____	____
7. I use my thoughts and attitudes to make my reality more life-affirming.[25]	____	____	____
8. Rather than worry about a problem when I can do nothing about it, I temporarily shelve it and get on with the matters at hand.	____	____	____
9. I approach life with the attitude that no problem is too big to confront, and some mysteries aren't meant to be solved.	____	____	____
10. I use my creative powers in many aspects of my life.	____	____	____

Total points for this section = ☐   ____ + ____ + ____

Divided by _____ (number of statements answered) = ____ Average score for this section.
(Transfer to the Wellness Inventory Wheel on **p. 3**)

Section 8 — Wellness and Playing/Working

	Yes, usually	Sometimes, maybe	No, rarely
	2	1	0
1. I enjoy expressing myself through art, dance, music, drama, sports, or other activities, and make time to do so.	____	____	____
2. I regularly exercise my creativity "muscles."	____	____	____
3. I enjoy spending time without planned or structured activities and make the effort to do so.	____	____	____
4. I can make much of my work into play.	____	____	____
5. At times I allow myself to do nothing.[26]	____	____	____
6. At times I can sleep late without feeling guilty.	____	____	____
7. The work I do is rewarding to me.	____	____	____
8. I am proud of my accomplishments.	____	____	____
9. I am playful and the people around me support my playfulness.	____	____	____
10. I have at least one activity, hobby, or sport that I enjoy regularly but do not feel compelled to do.	____	____	____

Total points for this section = ☐   ____ + ____ + ____

Divided by _____ (number of statements answered) = ____ Average score for this section.
(Transfer to the Wellness Inventory Wheel on **p. 3**)

---

[21] When you are unconscious of the content of your thoughts, they are more likely to control you. Observing them objectively develops self-awareness and strengthens your ability to take charge.

[22] Rather than trying to completely stop yourself from judging, you can observe your judgments as efforts by your ego to avoid getting on with life and hiding behind "right/wrong" game playing.

[23] Both biofeedback and the field of psycho-neuro-immunology have shown the connections between the mind, nervous system and body. The more you become consciously aware of that connection, the greater responsibility you can take for your health.

[24] Being aware of your internal distortion of perceptions can allow you to step back and reassess a situation more objectively.

[25] Honesty, tempered with care and concern, clears out many negative thoughts that can clutter up your mind, thus making your reality more fun. "Positive thinking" without honesty and truthfulness can backfire by suppressing valid concerns that must be addressed.

[26] Doing "nothing" can give us access to the more creative and nonverbal aspects of our being, so from another perspective, doing nothing becomes doing much more.

Section 9   Wellness and Communicating

	Yes, usually	Sometimes, maybe	No, rarely
	2	1	0
1. In conversation I can introduce a difficult topic and stay with it until I've gotten a satisfactory response from the other person.	____	____	____
2. I enjoy silence.	____	____	____
3. I am truthful and caring in my communications with others.	____	____	____
4. I assert myself (in a nonattacking manner) in an effort to be heard, rather than be passively resentful of others with whom I don't agree.[27]	____	____	____
5. I readily acknowledge my mistakes, apologizing for them if appropriate.	____	____	____
6. I am aware of my negative judgments of others and accept them as simply judgments—not necessarily truth.[28]	____	____	____
7. I am a good listener.	____	____	____
8. I am able to listen to people without interrupting them or finishing their sentences for them.	____	____	____
9. I can let go of my mental "labels" (for example, this is good, that is wrong) and judgmental attitudes about events in my life and see them in light of what they offer me.	____	____	____
10. I am aware when I play psychological "games" with those around me and work to be truthful and direct in my communications.[29]	____	____	____

Total points for this section = ☐   ____ + ____ + ____

Divided by ____ (number of statements answered) = ____ Average score for this section.
(Transfer to the Wellness Inventory Wheel on **p. 3**)

Section 10   Wellness and Sex

	Yes, usually	Sometimes, maybe	No, rarely
	2	1	0
1. I feel comfortable touching and exploring my body.	____	____	____
2. I think it's OK to masturbate if one chooses to do so.	____	____	____
3. My sexual education is adequate.	____	____	____
4. I feel good about the degree of closeness I have with men.	____	____	____
5. I feel good about the degree of closeness I have with women.	____	____	____
6. I am content with my level of sexual activity.[30]	____	____	____
7. I fully experience the many stages of lovemaking rather than focus only on orgasm.[31]	____	____	____
8. I desire to grow closer to some other people.	____	____	____
9. I am aware of the difference between needing someone and loving someone.	____	____	____
10. I am able to love others without dominating or being dominated by them.	____	____	____

Total points for this section = ☐   ____ + ____ + ____

Divided by ____ (number of statements answered) = ____ Average score for this section.
(Transfer to the Wellness Inventory Wheel on **p. 3**)

[27] Attacking others rarely accomplishes your goals in the long run. Persisting in your convictions without using force is more effective and usually solves the problem without creating new ones.
[28] It is important to recognize that our internal judgments of others are based on personal biases that often have little objective basis.
[29] Psychological games, defined by Eric Berne in *Games People Play*, are complex unconscious manipulations that result in the players getting negative attention and feeling bad about themselves.
[30] Including the choice to have no sexual activity.
[31] A common problem for many people is an overemphasis on performance and orgasm, rather than on enjoying a close sensual feeling with their partner whether or not they experience orgasm.

Section 11 Wellness and Finding Meaning

	Yes, usually	Sometimes, maybe	No, rarely
	2	1	0
1. I believe my life has direction and meaning.	____	____	____
2. My life is exciting and challenging.	____	____	____
3. I have goals in my life.	____	____	____
4. I am achieving my goals.	____	____	____
5. I look forward to the future as an opportunity for further growth.	____	____	____
6. I am able to talk about the death of someone close to me.	____	____	____
7. I am able to talk about my own death with family and friends.	____	____	____
8. I am prepared for my death.	____	____	____
9. I see my death as a step in my evolution.[32]	____	____	____
10. My daily life is a source of pleasure to me.	____	____	____

Total points for this section = ☐   ____ + ____ + ____

Divided by _____ (number of statements answered) = ____ Average score for this section.
(Transfer to the Wellness Inventory Wheel on **p. 3**)

This portion of the Inventory goes beyond the scope of most generally accepted "scientific" principles and expresses the values and beliefs of the authors. It is intended to stimulate interest in these areas. If you have strong beliefs to the contrary, you can skip the questions or make up your own.

Section 12 Wellness and Transcending

	Yes, usually	Sometimes, maybe	No, rarely
	2	1	0
1. I perceive problems as opportunities for growth.	____	____	____
2. I experience synchronistic events in my life (frequent "coincidences" seeming to have no cause-effect relationship).[33]	____	____	____
3. I believe there are dimensions of reality beyond verbal description or human comprehension.	____	____	____
4. At times I experience confusion and paradox in my search for understanding of the dimensions referred to above.	____	____	____
5. The concept of god has personal definition and meaning to me.	____	____	____
6. I experience a sense of wonder when I contemplate the universe.	____	____	____
7. I have abundant expectancy rather than specific expectations.	____	____	____
8. I allow others their beliefs without pressuring them to accept mine.	____	____	____
9. I use the messages interpreted from my dreams.	____	____	____
10. I enjoy practicing a spiritual discipline or allowing time to sense the presence of a greater force in guiding my passage through life.	____	____	____

Total points for this section = ☐   ____ + ____ + ____

Divided by _____ (number of statements answered) = ____ Average score for this section.
(Transfer to the Wellness Inventory Wheel on **p. 3**)

[32] Seeing your death as a stage of growth and preparing yourself consciously is an important part of finding meaning in your life.
[33] Modern physics reveals that the idea of cause and effect may be as limited as Newton's theory of a mechanical universe. It suggests that we must expand our view to see that everything in the universe is connected to everything else. (Synchronicity describes that experience.)

Part I

The following questions contain statements and their opposites. Notice that the statements extend from one extreme to the other. Where would you place yourself on this scale? Place a circle on the number that is most true for you at this time. Do not put your circles between numbers.

Life Purpose and Satisfaction

1. During most of the day,
my energy level is | very low | 1 2 3 4 5 6 7 | very high
2. As a whole, my life seems | dull | 1 2 3 4 5 6 7 | vibrant
3. My daily activities are | not a source of satisfaction | 1 2 3 4 5 6 7 | a source of satisfaction
4. I have come to expect that
every day will be | exactly the same | 1 2 3 4 5 6 7 | new and different
5. When I think deeply
about life | I do not feel there is any purpose to it | 1 2 3 4 5 6 7 | I feel there is a purpose to it
6. I feel that my life so far has | not been productive | 1 2 3 4 5 6 7 | been productive
7. I feel that the work*
I am doing | is of no value | 1 2 3 4 5 6 7 | is of great value
8. I wish I were different
than who I am. | agree strongly | 1 2 3 4 5 6 7 | disagree strongly
9. At this time, I have | no clearly defined goals for my life | 1 2 3 4 5 6 7 | clearly defined goals for my life
10. When sad things happen
to me or other people | I cannot feel positive about life | 1 2 3 4 5 6 7 | I continue to feel positive about life
11. When I think about what I
have done with my life, I feel | worthless | 1 2 3 4 5 6 7 | worthwhile
12. My present life | does not satisfy me | 1 2 3 4 5 6 7 | satisfies me
13. I feel joy in my heart | never | 1 2 3 4 5 6 7 | all the time
14. I feel trapped by the
circumstances of my life. | agree strongly | 1 2 3 4 5 6 7 | disagree strongly
15. When I think about my past | I feel many regrets | 1 2 3 4 5 6 7 | I feel no regrets
16. Deep inside myself | I do not feel loved | 1 2 3 4 5 6 7 | I feel loved
17. When I think about the
problems that I have | I do not feel hopeful about solving them | 1 2 3 4 5 6 7 | I feel very hopeful about solving them

*The definition of work is not limited to income-producing jobs. It includes childcare, housework, studies, and volunteer services.

Part II

Self-Confidence During Stress (answer according to how you feel during stressful times)

1. When there is a great deal of
pressure being placed on me | I get tense | 1 2 3 4 5 6 7 | I remain calm
2. I react to problems and difficulties | with a great deal of frustration | 1 2 3 4 5 6 7 | with no frustration
3. In a difficult situation, I am confident
that I will receive the help that I need. | disagree strongly | 1 2 3 4 5 6 7 | agree strongly
4. I experience anxiety | all the time | 1 2 3 4 5 6 7 | never
5. When I have made a mistake | I feel extreme dislike for myself | 1 2 3 4 5 6 7 | I continue to like myself
6. I find myself worrying that
something bad is going to happen
to me or those I love | all the time | 1 2 3 4 5 6 7 | never
7. In a stressful situation | I cannot concentrate easily | 1 2 3 4 5 6 7 | I can concentrate easily

11

(Continued)

8. I am fearful	all the time	1 2 3 4 5 6 7	never
9. When I need to stand up for myself	I cannot do it	1 2 3 4 5 6 7	I can do it easily
10. I feel less than adequate in most situations	agree strongly	1 2 3 4 5 6 7	disagree strongly
11. During times of stress, I feel isolated and alone.	agree strongly	1 2 3 4 5 6 7	disagree strongly
12. In really difficult situations	I feel unable to respond in positive ways	1 2 3 4 5 6 7	I feel able to respond in positive ways
13. When I need to relax	I experience no peace—only thoughts and worries	1 2 3 4 5 6 7	I experience a peacefulness—free of thoughts and worries
14. When I am frightened	I panic	1 2 3 4 5 6 7	I remain calm
15. I worry about the future	all the time	1 2 3 4 5 6 7	never

Scoring

The number you circled is your score for that question. Add your scores in each of the two sections and divide each sum by the number of questions in the section.

:: Life Purpose and Satisfaction: _____ ÷ 17 = ___.__

:: Self-Confidence During Stress: ___ ÷ 15 = ___.__

:: Combined Well-Being:

(add scores for both) _____ ÷ 32 = ___.__

Each score should range between 1.00 and 7.00 and may include decimals (for example 5.15).

Interpretation:

VERY LOW: 1.00 TO 2.49
MEDIUM LOW: 2.50 TO 3.99
MEDIUM HIGH: 4.00 TO 5.49
VERY HIGH: 5.50 TO 7.00

These scores reflect the strength with which you feel these positive emotions. Do they make sense to you? Review each scale and each question in each scale. Your score on each item gives you information about the emotions and areas in your life where your psychological resources are strong, as well as the areas where strength needs to be developed.

If you notice a large difference between the LPS and SCDS scores, use this information to recognize which central attitudes and aspects of your life most need strengthening. If your scores on both scales are very low, talk with a counselor or a friend about how you are feeling about yourself and your life.

Source: © 1989. Jared Kass. *Inventory of Positive Psychological Attitudes.* The Well-Being Scale is the self-test version of the Inventory of Positive Psychological Attitudes (IPPA-32) developed by Dr. Jared D. Kass. Reprinted with author's permission. For information, contact: Dr. Jared Kass, Division of Counseling and Psychology, Graduate School of Arts and Social Sciences, Lesley College, Cambridge, MA 02138.

Your Health Change Plan

for Psychological Wellness

Just as you can improve your physical well-being, you can enhance the state of your mind. Here are some suggestions:

:: Recognize and express your feelings. Pent-up emotions tend to fester inside, building into anger or depression.

:: Don't brood. Rather than merely mulling over a problem, try to find solutions that are positive and useful.

:: Take one step at a time. As long as you're taking some action to solve a problem, you can take pride in your ability to cope.

:: Spend more time doing those activities you know you do best. For example, if you are a good cook, prepare a meal for someone.

:: Separate what you do, especially any mistakes you make, from who you are. Instead of saying, "I'm so stupid," tell yourself, "That wasn't the smartest move I ever made, but I'll learn from it."

:: Use affirmations, positive statements that help reinforce the most positive aspects of your personality and experience. Every day, you might say, "I am a loving, caring person," or "I am honest and open in expressing my feelings." Write some affirmations of your own on index cards and flip through them occasionally.

:: List the things you would like to have or experience. Construct the statements as if you were already enjoying the situations you list, beginning each sentence with "I am." For example, "I am feeling great about doing well in my classes."

:: When your internal critic—the negative inner voice we all have—starts putting you down, force yourself to think of a situation that you handled well.

:: Set a limit on self-pity. Tell yourself, "I'm going to feel sorry for myself this morning, but this afternoon, I've got to get on with my life."

:: Volunteer. A third of Americans—some 89 million people—give of themselves through volunteer work. By doing the same, you may feel better too.

:: Exercise. In various studies around the world, physical exertion ranks as one of the best ways to change a bad mood, raise energy, and reduce tension.

Student Stress Scale

The Student Stress Scale, an adaptation of Holmes and Rahe's Life Events Scale for college-age adults, provides a rough indication of stress levels and possible health consequences.

In the Student Stress Scale, each event, such as beginning or ending school, is given a score that represents the amount of readjustment a person has to make as a result of the change. In some studies, using similar scales, people with serious illnesses have been found to have high scores.

To determine your stress score, add up the number of points corresponding to the events you have experienced in the past 12 months.

1.	Death of a close family member	100
2.	Death of a close friend	73
3.	Divorce of parents	65
4.	Jail term	63
5.	Major personal injury or illness	63
6.	Marriage	58
7.	Getting fired from a job	50
8.	Failing an important course	47
9.	Change in the health of a family member	45
10.	Pregnancy	45
11.	Sex problems	44
12.	Serious argument with a close friend	40
13.	Change in financial status	39
14.	Change of academic major	39
15.	Trouble with parents	39
16.	New girlfriend or boyfriend	37
17.	Increase in workload at school	37
18.	Outstanding personal achievement	36
19.	First quarter/semester in college	36
20.	Change in living conditions	31
21.	Serious argument with an instructor	30
22.	Getting lower grades than expected	29
23.	Change in sleeping habits	29
24.	Change in social activities	29
25.	Change in eating habits	28
26.	Chronic car trouble	26
27.	Change in number of family get-togethers	26
28.	Too many missed classes	25
29.	Changing colleges	24
30.	Dropping more than one class	23
31.	Minor traffic violations	20

Total Stress Score _____

Here's how to interpret your score: If your score is 300 or higher, you're at high risk for developing a health problem. If your score is between 150 and 300, you have a 50–50 chance of experiencing a serious health change within two years. If your score is below 150, you have a 1-in-3 chance of a serious health change.

Source: Kathleen Mullen and Gerald Costello. *Health Awareness Through Discovery.*

Your Health Change Plan

for Stress Management

:: **Strive for balance.** Review your commitments and plans, and if necessary, scale down.

:: **Get the facts.** When faced with a change or challenge, seek accurate information, which can bring vague fears down to earth.

:: **Talk with someone you trust.** A friend or a health professional can offer valuable perspective as well as psychological support.

:: **Exercise.** Even when your schedule gets jammed, carve out 20 or 30 minutes several times a week to walk, swim, bicycle, jog, or work out at the gym.

:: **Help others.** One of the most effective ways of dealing with stress is to find people in a worse situation and do something positive for them.

:: **Cultivate hobbies.** Pursuing a personal pleasure can distract you from the stressors in your life and help you relax.

:: **Master a form of relaxation.** Whether you choose meditation, yoga, mindfulness, or another technique, practice it regularly.

Physical Activity Stages of Change Questionnaire

For each of the following questions, please circle Yes or No. Please be sure to read the questions carefully.

Physical activity or exercise includes activities such as walking briskly, jogging, bicycling, swimming, or any other activity in which the exertion is at least as intense as these activities.

1) I am currently physically active. **NO YES**
2) I intend to become more physically active in the next 6 months. **NO YES**

For activity to be regular, it must add up to a total of 30 minutes or more per day and be done at least 5 days per week. For example, you could take one 30-minute walk or take three 10-minute walks for a daily total of 30 minutes.

3) I currently engage in regular physical activity. **NO YES**
4) I have been regularly physically active for the past 6 months. **NO YES**

Scoring Algorithm:

Precontemplation:	Question One = No
	Question Two = No
Contemplation:	Question One = No
	Question Two = Yes
Preparation:	Question One = Yes and
	Question Three = No
Action:	Question One = Yes
	Question Three = Yes and
	Question Four = No
Maintenance:	Question One = Yes
	Question Three = Yes
	Question Four = Yes

Sources: Bess Marcus and Beth Lewis. "Physical Activity and the Stages of Motivational Readiness for Change Model," *President's Council on Physical Fitness and Sports Research Digest*, Series 4, No. 1, March 2003, p. 1. H. Marcus and L. J. Forsyth. *Motivating People to Be Physically Active.* Champaign, Il.: Human Kinetics, 2003. Reprinted, by permission, from B. H. Marcus & L. H. Forsyth, 2003, *Motivating People to be Physically Active*, (Champaign, IL: Human Kinetics), 21.

Your Health Change Plan

for Physical Fitness

Once you know your stage of motivational readiness, you can employ the cognitive and behavioral strategies most likely to work for you now. As you progress through the stages of change, you can shift to other approaches. Here are some suggestions:

Precontemplation (not active and not thinking about becoming active)

:: Use this course as an opportunity to learn about the benefits of physical activity, including better mood, lower stress, stronger bones, and a lower risk of cardiovascular disease.

:: Set a small, reasonable goal that does not involve working up a sweat, such as looking up "exercise, benefits of" in the index of this book and reading the pages cited.

:: List what you see as the cons of physical activity. For example, do you fear it would take time you need for your studies? Think of small changes that don't require time, for instance, standing rather than sitting when talking on the phone, doing stretches while watching television, or taking a quick walk down the hall or up the stairs while waiting for a friend or a class to begin.

:: Identify barriers to physical activity, such as lack of money. Take advantage of your student status, and check out facilities, such as the swimming pool at the athletic center, or opportunities, such as an intramural soccer team, available to you free (or almost).

Contemplation (not active but thinking about becoming active)

:: Think back to activities you found enjoyable in the past. You might consider inline skating to class or around campus, or plan a hike for a weekend or school break.

:: Determine the types of activity you can realistically fit into your daily schedule. You might join friends for softball every Saturday, or sign up for an evening body-sculpting class.

:: Visualize success. Focus on the person you want to become: How would you look? What would you do differently? Find an image—from a magazine advertisement, for example—and post it where you can see it often.

:: Plan your rewards. Use a technique called shaping, which reinforces progress on the way to a goal. For instance, initially you might reward yourself once you engage in physical activity for 15 minutes a day. After a week, you get the reward only after 20 minutes a day. Over time you increase the number of days you are physically active as well as the number of minutes of activity per day.

(Continued)

:: Reach out for support. Find a friend, family member, or classmate who is willing or able to provide support for being active. Or join an organized martial arts class or an informal team.

Preparation (active but not at recommended levels)

:: Identify specific barriers that limit your activity. If your daily jogs are rained or snowed out, develop a list of indoor alternatives, such as walking stairs or working out to an exercise video.

:: Set specific daily and weekly goals. Your daily goal might begin with 10 or 15 minutes of activity. Your weekly goal might be to try a new activity, such as spinning or a dance class.

:: Divide physical activity over the course of the day with a 10 or 15 minute walk in the morning, another at lunch, and a third at the end of the day.

:: Document your progress. You could use a monthly calendar to keep track of the number of days you've exercised as well as the length of each workout. Or you can keep a more detailed record, noting the types of exercise you do every day, the intensity you work at, the duration of each workout, etc.

Action and Maintenance (active at recommended levels for less than six months)

:: Identify risk factors that might lead to relapse. If vacations or holiday breaks disrupt your routine, make a plan for alternative ways to remain active before you leave campus.

:: Stress proof your fitness program. In crunch times, you may feel you don't have time to spare for exercise. Multiple 10-minute walks during the day may be particularly useful both to keep up your fitness and to relieve stress buildup.

:: Avoid boredom. Think through ways to vary your exercise routine. Take different routes on your walks. Invite different friends to join you. Alternate working with free weights and resistance machines at the gym.

:: Set secondary goals. Once you've reached and maintained your goal for physical activity, set goals related to secondary benefits of exercise, for instance, losing weight or changing your body composition.

Take this readiness quiz to see if you're mentally ready before you begin a weight loss program. Mark each statement "true" or "false." Be honest with yourself! The answers should reflect the way you really think—not how you'd like to be!

1. I have thought a lot about my eating habits and physical activities, and I know what I might change.
2. I know that I need to make permanent, not temporary, changes in my eating and activity patterns.
3. I will feel successful only if I lose a lot of weight.
4. I know that it's best if I lose weight slowly.
5. I'm thinking about losing weight now because I really want to, not because someone else thinks I should.
6. I think losing weight would solve other problems in my life.
7. I am willing and able to increase my regular physical activity.
8. I can lose weight successfully only if I have no slip-ups.
9. I am willing to commit time and effort each week to organize and plan my food and activity choices.
10. Once I lose a few pounds but reach a plateau (I can't seem to lose more), I usually lose the motivation to keep going toward my weight goal.

11. I want to start a weight-loss program, even though my life is unusually stressful right now.

Now Score Yourself

Look at your answers for items 1, 2, 4, 5, 7, and 9. Score "1" if you answered "true" and "0" if you answered "false." For items 3, 6, 8, 10, and 11, score "0" for each "true" answer and "1" for each false answer.

No one score indicates if you're ready to start losing weight. But the higher your total score, the more likely you'll be successful.

If you scored 8 or higher, you probably have good reasons to lose weight now. And you know some of the steps that can help you succeed.

If you scored 5 to 7 points, you may need to reevaluate your reasons for losing weight and the strategies you'd follow.

If you scored 4 or less, now may not be the right time for you to lose weight. You may be successful initially, but you may not be able to sustain the effort to reach or maintain your weight goal. Reconsider your reasons and approach.

From America Dietetic Association's *Complete Food & Nutrition Guide,* 2/e by Rebecca Duyff. Copyright © 2002. Used by permission of John Wiley & Sons, Inc.

Your Health Change Plan

for Weight Loss

Any item you scored as "0" suggests a misconception about weight loss, or a problem area for you. So let's look at each item a bit more closely.

:: You can't change what you don't understand, and that includes your eating habits and activity pattern. Keep records for a week to pinpoint when, what, why, and how much you eat—as well as patterns and obstacles to regular physical activity.

:: You may be able to lose weight in the short run with drastic or highly restrictive changes in your eating habits or activity pattern. But they may be hard to live with permanently. Your food and activity plans should be healthful ones you can enjoy and sustain.

:: Many people fantasize about reaching a weight goal that's unrealistically low. If that sounds like you, rethink your meaning of success. A reasonable goal takes body type into consideration—and sets smaller, achievable "mile markers" along the way.

:: If you equate success with fast weight loss, you'll have problems keeping weight off. This "quick fix" attitude can backfire when you face the challenges of weight maintenance. The best and healthiest approach is to lose weight slowly while learning strategies to keep weight off permanently.

:: To be successful, the desire for and commitment to weight loss must come from you—not your best friend or a family member. People who lose weight, then keep it off, take responsibility for their weight goals and choose their own approach.

:: Being overweight may contribute to some social problems, but it's rarely the single cause. While body image and self-esteem are strongly linked, thinking you can solve all your problems by losing weight isn't realistic. And it may set you up for disappointment.

:: A habit of regular, moderate physical activity is a key factor to successfully losing weight—and keeping it off. For weight control, physical activity doesn't need to be strenuous to be effective. Any moderate physical activity that you enjoy and do regularly counts.

:: Most people don't expect perfection in their daily lives, yet they often feel they must stick to a weight-loss program perfectly. Perfection at weight loss isn't realistic. Rather than viewing lapses as catastrophes, see them as opportunities to find what triggers your problems and develop strategies for the future.

(Continued)

:: To successfully lose weight, you must take time to assess your problem areas, then develop the approach that's best for you. Success requires planning, commitment, and time.

:: First of all, a plateau in an ongoing weight-loss program is perfectly normal, so don't give up too soon! Before you lose your motivation, think about any past efforts that have failed, then identify strategies that can help you overcome those hurdles.

:: Weight loss itself can be a source of stress, so if you're already under stress, you may find a weight-loss program somewhat difficult to implement right now. Try to resolve other stressors in your life before starting your weight-loss effort.

Source: American Dietetic Association.

Effective, caring communication and loving affection markedly enhance a couple's relationship. The following self-test may help you to assess the degree of good communication, love, and respect in your intimate relationship. If you agree or mostly agree with a statement, answer yes. If you disagree or mostly disagree, answer no. You may wish to have your partner respond to this assessment as well. If so, mark your answers on a separate sheet.

1. My partner seeks out my opinion.   Yes   No
2. My partner cares about my feelings.   Yes   No
3. I don't feel ignored very often.   Yes   No
4. We touch each other a lot.   Yes   No
5. We listen to each other.   Yes   No
6. We respect each other's ideas.   Yes   No
7. We are affectionate toward one another.   Yes   No
8. I feel my partner takes good care of me.   Yes   No
9. What I say counts.   Yes   No
10. I am important in our decisions.   Yes   No
11. There's lots of love in our relationship.   Yes   No
12. We are genuinely interested in
    one another.   Yes   No
13. I love spending time with my partner.   Yes   No
14. We are very good friends.   Yes   No
15. Even during rough times, we can
    be empathetic.   Yes   No
16. My partner is considerate of
    my viewpoint.   Yes   No
17. My partner finds me physically
    attractive.   Yes   No
18. My partner expresses warmth
    toward me.   Yes   No
19. I feel included in my partner's life.   Yes   No
20. My partner admires me.   Yes   No

Scoring:

A preponderance of yes answers indicates that you enjoy a strong relationship characterized by good communication and loving affection. If you answered yes to fewer than seven items, it is likely that you are not feeling loved and respected and that the communication in your relationship is decidedly lacking.

Source: Reprinted with the permission of Simon & Schuster Adult Publishing Group, from *Why Marriages Succeed or Fail: What You Can Learn From the Breakthrough Research to Make Your Marriage Last*, by John Gottman, Ph.D. Copyright © 1994 by John Gottman. All rights reserved.

Your Health Change Plan

for Better Communication

Like other skills, communication improves with practice. Here are some suggestions that can enhance your ability to express yourself more precisely and to understand spoken and unspoken messages from others.

:: *Tune into your body talk.* Notice details about the way you speak, gesture, and move. If possible, watch yourself on videotape. Analyze the emotions you're feeling at the time and think of how they may be influencing your body language.

:: *Learn to establish good eye contact, but don't glare or stare.* If you sense that someone feels uncomfortable with an intense eye grip, shift your focus so that your gaze hits somewhere between the eyes and the chin, rather than pupil-to-pupil.

:: *Avoid putting up barriers.* If you fold your arms across your chest, you'll look defensive or uninterested in contact. Crossing your legs or ankles also can seem like a way of keeping your distance.

:: *Identify the little things you characteristically do when you're tense.* Some people pat their hair or pick at their ears; others rub their necks, twist a ring or watch, twirl a lock of hair, or play with a pen. Train yourself to become aware of what you're doing (have a friend give your a signal, if necessary) and to control your mannerisms.

:: *Use "I" statements.* Describe what's going on with you. Say, "I worry about being liked" or "I get frustrated when I can't put my feelings into words." Avoid generalities such as "You never think about my feelings," or "Nobody understands me."

:: *Gently ask how the other person feels.* If your friend or partner describes thoughts rather than feelings, ask for more adjectives. Was he or she sad, excited, angry, hurt?

:: *Become a very good listener.* When another person talks, don't interrupt, ask why, judge, or challenge. Nod your head. Use your body language and facial expression to show you're eager to hear more.

:: *Respect confidences.* Treat a friend's or partner's secrets with the discretion they deserve. Consider them a special gift entrusted to your care.

Mark each of the following statements True or False:

1. Men and women have completely different sex hormones.
2. Premenstrual syndrome (PMS) is primarily a psychological problem.
3. Circumcision diminishes a man's sexual pleasure.
4. Sexual orientation may have a biological basis.
5. Masturbation is a sign of emotional immaturity.
6. Only homosexual men engage in anal intercourse.
7. Despite their awareness of AIDS, many college students do not practice safe sex.
8. After age 60, lovemaking is mainly a fond memory, not a regular pleasure of daily living.
9. Doctors advise against having intercourse during a woman's menstrual period.
10. Only men ejaculate.
11. It is possible to be infected with HIV during a single sexual encounter.
12. Impotence is always a sign of emotional or sexual problems in a relationship.

Answers:

1. False. Men and women have the same hormones, but in different amounts.
2. False. PMS has been recognized as a physiological disorder that may be caused by a hormonal deficiency, abnormal levels of thyroid hormone, or social and environmental factors, such as stress.

3. False. Sex therapists have not been able to document differences in sensitivity to stimulation between circumcised and uncircumcised men.
4. True. Researchers documented structural differences in the brains of homosexual men and women.
5. False. Throughout a person's life, masturbation can be a form of sexual release and pleasure.
6. False. As many as one in every four married couples under age 35 have reported that they occasionally engage in anal intercourse.
7. True. In one recent study, more than a third of college students had engaged in vaginal or anal intercourse at least once in the previous year without using effective protection from conception or sexually transmitted infections (STIs).
8. False. More than a third of American married men and women older than 60 make love at least once a week as do 10% of those older than 70.
9. False. There's no medical reason to avoid intercourse during a woman's menstrual period.
10. False. Stimulation of the Grafenberg spot in a woman's vagina may lead to a release of fluid from her urethra during orgasm.
11. True. Although the risk increases with repeated sexual contact with an infected partner, an individual can contract HIV during a single sexual encounter.
12. False. Many erection difficulties have physical causes.

Your Health Change Plan

for Responsible Sexuality

Your score on this self-survey may indicate that you know a lot more—or less—about sex than you thought you did. Part of sexual responsibility is being informed about sexuality, including reproductive anatomy, sexual orientation, the range of sexual behaviors, and ways of protecting yourself from sexually transmitted diseases.

The Sexuality Information and Education Council of the United States (SIECUS) has worked with nongovernmental organizations around the world to develop a consensus about the life behaviors of a sexually healthy and responsible adult. These include:

:: Appreciating one's own body.

:: Seeking information about reproduction as needed.

:: Affirming that sexual development may or may not include reproduction or genital sexual experience.

:: Interacting with both genders in respectful and appropriate ways.

:: Affirming one's own sexual orientation and respecting the sexual orientation of others.

:: Expressing love and intimacy in appropriate ways.

:: Developing and maintaining meaningful relationships.

:: Avoiding exploitative or manipulative relationships.

:: Making informed choices about family options and lifestyles.

:: Enjoying and expressing one's sexuality throughout life.

:: Expressing one's sexuality in ways congruent with one's values.

:: Discriminating between life-enhancing sexual behaviors and those that are harmful to self and/or others.

:: Expressing one's sexuality while respecting the rights of others.

:: Seeking new information to enhance one's sexuality.

:: Using contraception effectively to avoid unintended pregnancy.

:: Preventing sexual abuse.

:: Seeking early prenatal care.

:: Avoiding contracting or transmitting a sexually transmitted infection, including HIV.

(Continued)

:: Practicing health-promoting behaviors, such as regular checkups, breast and testicular self-exam, and early identification of potential problems.

:: Demonstrating tolerance for people with different sexual values and lifestyles.

:: Exercising democratic responsibility to influence legislation dealing with sexual issues.

:: Assessing the impact of family, cultural, religious, media, and societal messages on one's thoughts, feelings, values, and behaviors related to sexuality.

:: Promoting the rights of all people to accurate sexuality information.

:: Avoiding behaviors that exhibit prejudice and bigotry.

:: Rejecting stereotypes about the sexuality of diverse populations.

Which Contraceptive Method Is Best for You?

Answer yes or no to each statement as it applies to you and, if appropriate, your partner.

1. You have high blood pressure or cardiovascular disease.
2. You smoke cigarettes.
3. You have a new sexual partner.
4. An unwanted pregnancy would be devastating to you.
5. You have a good memory.
6. You or your partner have multiple sexual partners.
7. You prefer a method with little or no bother.
8. You have heavy, crampy periods.
9. You need protection against STIs.
10. You are concerned about endometrial and ovarian cancer.
11. You are forgetful.
12. You need a method right away.
13. You're comfortable touching your own and your partner's genitals.
14. You have a cooperative partner.
15. You like a little extra vaginal lubrication.
16. You have sex at unpredictable times and places.
17. You are in a monogamous relationship and have at least one child.

Scoring:

Recommendations are based on Yes answers to the following numbered statements:

The combination pill: 4, 5, 6, 8, 10, 16
The progestin-only pill: 1, 2, 5, 7, 16
The patch: 4, 7, 8, 11, 16
The NuvaRing: 4, 7, 8, 11, 13, 16
Condoms: 1, 2, 3, 6, 9, 12, 13, 14
Depo-Provera: 1, 2, 4, 7, 11, 16
Lunelle: 4, 7, 11, 16
Diaphragm, cervical cap, or FemCap: 1, 2, 13, 14
Mirena IUD: 1, 2, 7, 8, 11, 13, 16, 17
Copper T IUD: 1, 2, 7, 11, 13, 16, 17
Spermicides: 1, 2, 12, 13, 14, 15
Sponge: 1, 2, 12, 13

Your Health Change Plan

for Choosing a Contraceptive

Your responses may indicate that there's more than one appropriate method of birth control for you. Remember that you may choose different types of birth control at different stages of your life, or switch contraceptives for various reasons. You and your partner should always consider and discuss these factors:

:: **Effectiveness.** Keep in mind that your own conscientiousness will play an important role. If you forget to take your daily pill, or if you decide not to use a condom "just this once," you'll increase the odds of pregnancy by interfering with effective birth control.

:: **Suitability.** If you don't have sex very often, a contraceptive with many risks and side effects, such as the pill, may be wrong for you. If you have many sexual partners and are at risk of contracting a sexually transmitted infection, a condom may provide protection against pregnancy and infection, especially if used with a diaphragm or cervical cap.

:: **Side effects.** Some complications related to contraceptives are serious health threats. Be sure to ask questions and gather as much information as possible about what side effects to expect.

:: **Safety.** The risks of certain contraceptives, such as the pill, may be too great to allow their use, if, for example, you have high blood pressure. Be honest in describing your medical history to your physician.

:: **Future fertility.** Some women don't return to regular menstrual cycles for six months to a year after discontinuing oral contraceptives. This possibility may or may not be important to you now, but you should try to look ahead.

:: **Cost.** The only free contraceptive methods are abstinence and rhythm methods. If you're on a tight budget, you might consider the relative costs of a year's prescription of oral contraceptives compared to a year's supply of condoms or spermicidal foam or jelly. You should also think about the long-term costs and consequences.

:: **Reduced risk of sexually transmitted infections.** Some forms of contraception, in particular barrier contraceptives and spermicides, help reduce the risk of transmission of some STIs. However, none provides complete protection.

Individuals with a substance dependence or abuse disorder may

:: Use more of an illegal drug or a prescription medication or use a drug for a longer period of time than they desire or intend. _____

:: Try, repeatedly and unsuccessfully, to cut down or control their drug use. _____

:: Spend a great deal of time doing whatever is necessary in order to get drugs, taking them, or recovering from their use. _____

:: Be so high or feel so bad after drug use that they often cannot do their job or fulfill other responsibilities. _____

:: Give up or cut back on important social, work, or recreational activities because of drug use. _____

:: Continue to use drugs even though they realize that they are causing or worsening physical or mental problems. _____

:: Use a lot more of a drug in order to achieve a "high" or desired effect or feel fewer such effects than in the past. _____

:: Use drugs in dangerous ways or situations. _____

:: Have repeated drug-related legal problems, such as arrests for possession. _____

:: Continue to use drugs, even though the drug causes or worsens social or personal problems, such as arguments with a spouse. _____

:: Develop hand tremors or other withdrawal symptoms if they cut down or stop drug use. _____

:: Take drugs to relieve or avoid withdrawal symptoms. _____

The more blanks that you or someone close to you checks, the more reason you have to be concerned about drug use. The most difficult step for anyone with a substance use disorder is to admit that he or she has a problem. Sometimes a drug-related crisis, such as being arrested or fired, forces individuals to acknowledge the impact of drugs. If not, those who care—family, friends, boss, physician—may have to confront them and insist that they do something about it. This confrontation, planned beforehand, is called an *intervention* and can be the turning point for drug users and their families.

Your Health Change Plan

for Recognizing Substance Abuse

How can you tell if a friend or loved one has a substance use disorder? Look for the following warning signs:

:: **An abrupt change in attitude.** Individuals may lose interest in activities they once enjoyed or in being with friends they once valued.

:: **Mood swings.** Drug users may often seem withdrawn or "out of it," or they may display unusual temper flareups.

:: **A decline in performance.** Students may start skipping classes, stop studying, or not complete assignments; their grades may plummet.

:: **Increased sensitivity.** Individuals may react intensely to any criticism or become easily frustrated or angered.

:: **Secrecy.** Drug users may make furtive telephone calls or demand greater privacy concerning their personal possessions or their whereabouts.

:: **Physical changes.** Individuals using drugs may change their pattern of sleep, spending more time in bed or sleeping at odd hours. They also may change their eating habits and lose weight.

:: **Money problems.** Drug users may constantly borrow money, seem short of cash, or begin stealing.

:: **Changes in appearance.** As they become more involved with drugs, users often lose regard for their personal appearance and look disheveled.

:: **Defiance of restrictions.** Individuals may ignore or deliberately refuse to comply with deadlines, curfews, or other regulations.

:: **Changes in relationships.** Drug users may quarrel more frequently with family members or old friends and develop new, strong allegiances with new acquaintances, including other drug users.

This self-assessment, the Michigan Alcoholism Screening Test (MAST), is widely used to identify potential problems. This test screens for the major psychological, sociological, and physiological consequences of alcoholism.

To complete it, simply answer Yes or No to the following questions, and add up the points shown in the right column for your answers.

	Yes	No	Points
1. Do you enjoy a drink now and then?			(0 for either)
2. Do you think that you're a normal drinker? (By normal, we mean that you drink less than or as much as most other people.)			(2 for no)
3. Have you ever awakened the morning after some drinking the night before and found that you couldn't remember part of the evening?			(2 for yes)
4. Does your wife, husband, a parent, or other near relative ever worry or complain about your drinking?			(1 for yes)
5. Can you stop drinking without a struggle after one or two drinks?			(2 for no)
6. Do you ever feel guilty about your drinking?			(1 for yes)
7. Do friends or relatives think that you're a normal drinker?			(2 for no)
8. Do you ever try to limit your drinking to certain times of the day or to certain places?			(0 for either)
9. Have you ever attended a meeting of Alcoholics Anonymous?			(2 for yes)
10. Have you ever gotten into physical fights when drinking?			(1 for yes)
11. Has your drinking ever created problems for you and your wife, husband, a parent, or other relative?			(2 for yes)
12. Has your wife, husband, or other family members ever gone to anyone for help about your drinking?			(2 for yes)
13. Have you ever lost friends because of your drinking?			(2 for yes)
14. Have you ever gotten into trouble at work or school because of your drinking?			(2 for yes)
15. Have you ever lost a job because of your drinking?			(2 for yes)

	Yes	No	Points
16. Have you ever neglected your obligations, your family, or your work for two or more days in a row because of drinking?			(2 for yes)
17. Do you drink before noon fairly often?			(1 for yes)
18. Have you ever been told you have liver trouble? cirrhosis?			(2 for yes)
19. After heavy drinking, have you ever had delirium tremens (DTs) or severe shaking, or heard voices or seen things that weren't actually there?			(2 for yes*)
20. Have you ever gone to anyone for help about your drinking?			(5 for yes)
21. Have you ever been in a hospital because of your drinking?			(5 for yes)
22. Have you ever been a patient in a psychiatric hospital or on a psychiatric ward of a general hospital where drinking was part of the problem that resulted in hospitalization?			(2 for yes)
23. Have you ever been seen at a psychiatric or mental health clinic or gone to any doctor, social worker, or clergyman for help with any emotional problem where drinking was part of the problem?			(2 for yes)
24. Have you ever been arrested for drunk driving, driving while intoxicated, or driving under the influence of alcoholic beverages?			(2 for yes)
25. Have you ever been arrested, or taken into custody, even for a few hours, because of drunken behavior? (If Yes, How many times? _____**)			(2 for yes)

*Five points for delirium tremens

**Two points for each arrest

Scoring:

In general, five or more points places you in an alcoholic category; four points suggests alcoholism; while three or fewer points indicates that you're *not* alcoholic.

(Continued)

Your Health Change Plan

for Responsible Drinking

:: **Don't drink alone.** Cultivate friendships with non-drinkers and responsible moderate drinkers.

:: **Don't use alcohol as a medicine.** Rather than reaching for a drink to put you to sleep, help you relax, or relieve tension, develop alternative means of unwinding, such as exercise, meditation, or listening to music.

:: **Develop a party plan.** Set a limit on how many drinks you'll have before you go out—and stick to it.

:: **Alternate alcoholic and nonalcoholic drinks.** At a social occasion, have a nonalcoholic beverage to quench your thirst.

:: **Drink slowly.** Never have more than one drink an hour.

:: **Eat before and while drinking.** Choose foods high in protein (cheese, meat, eggs, or milk) rather than salty foods, like peanuts or chips, that increase thirst.

:: **Be wary of mixed drinks.** Fizzy mixers, like club soda and ginger ale, speed alcohol to the blood and brain.

:: **Don't make drinking the primary focus of any get-together.** Cultivate other interests and activities that you can enjoy on your own or with friends.

:: **Learn to say no.** A simple "Thank you, but I've had enough" will do.

:: **Stay safe.** During or after drinking, avoid any tasks, including driving, that could be affected by alcohol.

Answer the following questions as honestly as you can by placing a check mark in the appropriate column:

	Yes	No
1. Do you smoke every day?	__	__
2. Do you smoke because of shyness and to build up self-confidence?	__	__
3. Do you smoke to escape from boredom and worries or while under pressure?	__	__
4. Have you ever burned a hole in your clothes, carpet, furniture, or car with a cigarette?	__	__
5. Have you ever had to go to the store late at night or at another inconvenient time because you were out of cigarettes?	__	__
6. Do you feel defensive or angry when people tell you that your smoke is bothering them?	__	__
7. Has a doctor or dentist ever suggested that you stop smoking?	__	__
8. Have you ever promised someone that you would stop smoking, then broken your promise?	__	__
9. Have you ever felt physical or emotional discomfort when trying to quit?	__	__
10. Have you ever successfully stopped smoking for a period of time, only to start again?	__	__
11. Do you buy extra supplies of tobacco to make sure you won't run out?	__	__
12. Do you find it difficult to imagine life without smoking?	__	__

	Yes	No
13. Do you choose only those activities and entertainments during which you can smoke?	__	__
14. Do you prefer, seek out, or feel more comfortable in the company of smokers?	__	__
15. Do you inwardly despise or feel ashamed of yourself because of your smoking?	__	__
16. Do you ever find yourself lighting up without having consciously decided to?	__	__
17. Has your smoking ever caused trouble at home or in a relationship?	__	__
18. Do you ever tell yourself that you can stop smoking whenever you want to?	__	__
19. Have you ever felt that your life would be better if you didn't smoke?	__	__
20. Do you continue to smoke even though you are aware of the health hazards posed by smoking?	__	__

If you answered Yes to one or two of these questions, there's a chance that you are addicted or are becoming addicted to nicotine. If you answered Yes to three or more of these questions, you are probably already addicted to nicotine.

Source: Nicotine Anonymous World Services, San Francisco.

Your Health Change Plan

for Kicking the Habit

Here's a six-point program to help you or someone you love quit smoking. (*Caution:* Don't undertake the quit-smoking program until you have a two- to four-week period of relatively unstressful work and study schedules or social commitments.)

1. *Identify your smoking habits.* Keep a daily diary (a piece of paper wrapped around your cigarette pack with a rubber band will do) and record the time you smoke, the activity associated with smoking (after breakfast, in the car), and your urge for a cigarette (desperate, pleasant, or automatic). For the first week or two, don't bother trying to cut down; just use the diary to learn the conditions under which you smoke.

2. *Get support.* It can be tough to go it alone. Phone your local chapter of the American Cancer Society, or otherwise get the names of some ex-smokers who can give you support.

3. *Begin by tapering off.* For a period of one to four weeks, aim at cutting down to, say, 12 or 15 cigarettes a day; or change to a lower-nicotine brand, and concentrate on not increasing the number of cigarettes you smoke. As indicated by your diary, begin by cutting out those cigarettes you smoke automatically. In addition, restrict the times you allow yourself to smoke. Throughout this period, stay in touch, once a day or every few days, with your ex-smoker friend(s) to discuss your problems.

4. *Set a quit date.* At some point during the tapering-off period, announce to everyone—friends, family, and ex-smokers—when you're going to quit. Do it with flair. Announce it to coincide with a significant date, such as your birthday or anniversary.

5. *Stop.* A week before Q-day, smoke only five cigarettes a day. Begin late in the day, say after 4:00 P.M. Smoke the first two cigarettes in close succession. Then, in the evening, smoke the last three, also in close succession,

(Continued)

about 15 minutes apart. Focus on the negative aspects of cigarettes, such as the rawness in your throat and lungs. After seven days, quit and give yourself a big reward on that day, such as a movie or a fantastic meal or new clothes.

6. *Follow up.* Stay in touch with your ex-smoker friend(s) during the following two weeks, particularly if anything stressful or tense occurs that might trigger a

return to smoking. Think of the person you're becoming—the very person cigarette ads would have you believe smoking makes you. Now that you're quitting smoking, you're becoming healthier, sexier, more sophisticated, more mature, and better looking—and you've earned it!

Sources: American Cancer Society; National Cancer Institute.

1. Which of the following STIs can be transmitted EVEN when you use a condom?
   a. chlamydia
   b. HIV
   c. gonorrhea
   d. genital warts
2. True or False: Cold sores and genital herpes are not the same thing, so oral sex is safe when my partner has a cold sore.
   True
   False
3. Hepatitis B is ___ times more infectious than HIV.
   a. 20
   b. 100
   c. 50
   d. 10
4. The STI below is known as the "silent" epidemic.
   a. HIV
   b. genital herpes
   c. chlamydia
   d. public lice ("crabs")
5. True or False: It's estimated that at least half of all new HIV infections in the United States are among people under 25.
   True
   False
6. What do Pope Alexander VI, Ivan the Terrible, Henry VIII, and Al Capone have in common?
   a. They all lost their virginity after the age of 30.
   b. They all had taken a vow of celibacy.
   c. They all died virgins.
   d. They all died of syphillis.
7. By age 24, at least one in ___ sexually active people will have contracted an STI.
   a. 10
   b. 20
   c. 3
   d. 5
8. True or False: "My girlfriend has a Pap smear every year, so I know I'm clean."
   True
   False
9. It takes up to ___ months for people infected with HIV to develop enough antibodies for their HIV status to be accurately detected by testing.
   a. 6
   b. 12
   c. 3
   d. 9
10. True or False: You are doomed, you may as well walk around in a latex bodysuit and never touch another person again!
    True
    False

Source: www.smartersex.org/quizzes/sti_quiz.asp Copyright 2002 SmarterSex.org.

Scoring:

Question 1: d. genital warts
Unlike the other three infections, genital warts, caused by certain strains of the human papilloma virus, are transmitted by direct skin-to-skin contact. If your partner has a genital wart on an exposed area and your skin comes in contact with it, transmission is likely. Even scarier, HPV is one of the most common STIs among young, sexually active people, with an estimated 5.5 million people becoming infected with HPV each year. Using condoms is still a good idea though, because condom use may reduce exposure to HPV. Like all STIs, the best way to prevent infection is to limit your number of sex partners, practice sexual abstinence, and avoid sexual contact if you think your partner is infected.

Question 2: False
Absolutely not! The herpes simplex virus (HSV) 1 and 2 look similar and either one can infect the mouth or genitals. Usually, HSV-1 occurs above the waist and HSV-2 occurs below the waist, but it is possible that HSV-1 can cause genital herpes. Herpes is a lifelong disease once infected, so it's not worth the risk! Because the virus can linger in body fluids long after a sore is gone, if you or your partner have either type of herpes the absolute best protection is to use dental dams or condoms every time you have sex or oral sex.

Question 3: b. 100
Yep, Hepatitis B is 100 times more infectious than HIV. Hepatitis B is a viral disease that attacks the liver and can cause extreme illness, even death. But the good news is that this is a 100-percent preventable disease! There is a safe and effective vaccine against hepatitis B, which is usually available at your student health center. This is the only STI vaccine that you can protect yourself with, so what are you waiting for?

Question 4: c. chlamydia
Crabs may be silent, but chlamydia is considered to be the "silent" epidemic because three-quarters of women and half of men with the disease have no symptoms. Possible symptoms include discharge from the penis or vagina and a

(Continued)

33

burning sensation when urinating. This "silent" epidemic can lead to devastating results if untreated. Genital chlamydia can cause preventable infertility and ectopic pregnancy.

Question 5: True
This means that every hour, two Americans between the ages of 13 and 24 contract HIV. In 2002, the Centers for Disease Control report that there have been 27,880 cases of AIDS reported for people in the U.S. aged 20–24. This includes college students. It's important to realize that AIDS is an epidemic that affects everyone, not just IV-drug users and promiscuous homosexuals. The only way to protect yourself is to use a condom EVERY time. It's just that simple.

Question 6: They all died of syphilis.
These guys don't just have fame in common—they also all died from syphilis. HIV and Hepatitis B aren't the only deadly STIs. Syphilis progresses in stages, and during the first stage, a single sore may appear on the genitals or mouth, but often there are no symptoms. If untreated, the symptoms may disappear, but the infection stays in the body and progresses into the third stage, causing damage to the brain, heart, and nervous system, and even death.

Question 7: c. 3
There are approximately 10 million new cases of STIs each year among people aged 15–24 in the United States; that means that one in three sexually active people will have contracted an STI by age 24. So you can't go by looks, clothes, or how much money somebody has to determine if they have an STI. Remember, you're not just having sex with that person, but with everyone they've slept with, and everyone they've slept with . . . .

Question 8: False
Many people assume STI screening is a standard part of a routine Pap smear, but it isn't. Men and women should have yearly physical exams, and at that time should ask their doctor to screen them for STIs. This may seem like common sense, but getting screened through your partner does not mean you're safe. Not everyone develops an STI when exposed, so it's important you get tested.

Question 9: a. 6
A negative HIV result means that no HIV antibodies were found at the time that the blood was drawn. In most instances that means a person does not have HIV; however, it might mean you were tested too soon after infection. Your best bet is to get tested every six months, just to make sure. It's better to know now and get treated, than not know and infect people you love.

Question 10: False
Yes, sex can be scary these days, but it doesn't mean you can't enjoy yourself. If you are responsible about using a condom EVERY time you have intercourse, the chances of ending up with something nasty are slim. Free love comes with a price, one that you won't have to pay if you act responsibly. If you make STI screening a routine part of your physical, know your partner's status, and use a condom and dental dam every time you have sex, you are doing "it" right!

Your Health Change Plan

for Coping with STIs

More than 25 infections are spread by sexual activity. Here are some practical steps that reduce—but do not eliminate—the risks as well as recommendations for what to do if you contract a sexually transmitted infection and for informing a potential partner:

What You Can Do to Lower the Risk
::   Use a new condom each and every time you engage in any form of intercourse. Men should try different brands to find the ones they like best.

::   When putting on a condom, men should pinch its tip as they unroll it (all the way down!) to prevent an air bubble from forming in the reservoir tip. They must hold onto the base of their condom as they withdraw so it doesn't slip off.

::   Do not use spermicide containing nonoxynol-9. Contrary to past advice, experts now advise against choosing safer sex products with nonoxynol-9. According to recent research, nonoxynol-9 without condoms is ineffective against HIV transmission. Even with condoms, it does not protect women from the bacteria that cause gonorrhea and chlamydia.

::   If a condom fails during vaginal or anal intercourse, remove it.

::   After potential exposure to an STI, men may give themselves a little extra protection by urinating and washing their genitals with an antibacterial soap.

::   Oral sex can transmit various STIs, including herpes, gonorrhea, syphilis, and HIV. Safer-sex barriers, including latex condoms (without nonoxynol-9) for fellatio and either saran wrap or **dental dams** for cunnilingus, can lower the risk.

::   Because bacteria can be transmitted by hand, wash your hands with hot water and antibacterial soap after sex.

(Continued)

What to Do If You Have an STI

:: If you suspect that you have an STI, don't feel too embarrassed to get help through a physician's office or a clinic. Treatment relieves discomfort, prevents complications, and halts the spread of the disease.

:: Following diagnosis, take oral medication (which may be given instead of or in addition to shots) exactly as prescribed.

:: Try to figure out from whom you got the STI. Be sure to inform that person, who may not be aware of the problem.

:: If you have an STI, never deceive a prospective partner about it. Tell the truth—simply and clearly. Be sure your partner understands exactly what you have and what the risks are.

Telling a Partner You Have an STI

Even though the conversation can be awkward and embarrassing, you need to talk honestly about any STI that you may have been exposed to or contracted. What you don't say can be hazardous to your partner's health. Here are some guidelines:

:: ***Talk before you become intimate.*** A good way to start is simply by saying, *"There is something we need to talk over first."*

:: ***Be honest.*** Don't downplay any potential risks.

:: ***Don't blame.*** Even if you suspect that your partner was the source of your infection, focus on the need for medical attention.

:: ***Be sensitive to your partner's feelings.*** Anger and resentment are common reactions when someone feels at risk. Try to listen without becoming defensive.

:: ***Seek medical attention.*** Do not engage in sexual intimacies until you obtain a doctor's assurance that you are no longer contagious.

Source: From www.smartersex.org/quizzes/sti_quiz.asp. Copyright 2002 SmarterSex.org. Used with permission from Bacchus and Gamma Peer Education Network.

Instructions

Test your knowledge about high blood cholesterol. Mark each statement true or false.

1. High blood cholesterol is one of the risk factors for heart disease that you can do something about. _____
2. To lower your blood cholesterol level, you must stop eating meat altogether. _____
3. Any blood cholesterol level below 240 mg/dL is desirable for adults. _____
4. Fish oil supplements are recommended to lower blood cholesterol. _____
5. To lower your blood cholesterol level, you should eat less saturated fat, total fat, and cholesterol, and lose weight if you are overweight. _____
6. Saturated fats raise your blood cholesterol levels more than anything else in your diet. _____
7. All vegetable oils help lower blood cholesterol levels. _____
8. Lowering blood cholesterol levels can help people who have already had a heart attack. _____
9. All children need to have their blood cholesterol levels checked. _____
10. Women don't need to worry about high blood cholesterol and heart disease. _____
11. Reading food labels can help you eat the heart healthy way. _____

Answers

1. True. High blood cholesterol is one of the risk factors for heart disease that a person can do something about. High blood pressure, cigarette smoking, diabetes, being overweight, and physical inactivity are the others.
2. False. Although some red meat is high in saturated fat and cholesterol, which can raise your blood cholesterol, you do not need to stop eating it or any other single food. Red meat is an important source of protein, iron, and other vitamins and minerals. You should, however, cut back on the amount of saturated fat and cholesterol that you eat. One way to do this is by choosing lean cuts of meat with the fat trimmed. Another way is to watch your portion sizes and eat no more than 6 ounces of meat a day. Six ounces is about the size of two decks of playing cards.
3. False. A total blood cholesterol level under 200 mg/dL is desirable and usually puts you at a lower risk for heart disease. A blood cholesterol level of 240 mg/dL is high and increases your risk of heart disease. If your cholesterol level is high, your doctor will want to check your level of LDL-cholesterol ("bad" cholesterol). A *high* level of LDL-cholesterol increases your

risk of heart disease, as does a *low* level of HDL-cholesterol ("good" cholesterol). An HDL-cholesterol level below 35 mg/dL is considered a risk factor for heart disease. A total cholesterol level of 200–239 mg/dL is considered borderline-high and usually increases your risk for heart disease. All adults 20 years of age or older should have their blood cholesterol level checked at least once every five years.

4. False. Fish oils are a source of omega-3 fatty acids, which are a type of polyunsaturated fat. Fish oil supplements generally do not reduce blood cholesterol levels. Also, the effect of the long-term use of fish oil supplements is not known. However, fish is a good food choice because it is low in saturated fat.
5. True. Eating less fat, especially saturated fat, and cholesterol can lower your blood cholesterol level. Generally your blood cholesterol level should begin to drop a few weeks after you start on a cholesterol-lowering diet. How much your level drops depends on the amounts of saturated fat and cholesterol you used to eat, how high your blood cholesterol is, how much weight you lose if you are overweight, and how your body responds to the changes you make. Over time, you may reduce your blood cholesterol level by 10–50 mg/dL or even more.
6. True. Saturated fats raise your blood cholesterol level more than anything else. So, the best way to reduce your cholesterol level is to cut back on the amount of saturated fats that you eat. These fats are found in largest amounts in animal products such as butter, cheese, whole milk, ice cream, cream, and fatty meats. They are also found in some vegetable oils—coconut, palm, and palm kernel oils.
7. False. Most vegetable oils—canola, corn, olive, safflower, soybean, and sunflower oils—contain mostly monounsaturated and polyunsaturated fats, which help lower blood cholesterol when used in place of saturated fats. However a few vegetable oils—coconut, palm, and palm kernel oils—contain more saturated fat than unsaturated fat. Limit the total amount of any fats or oils, since even those that are unsaturated are rich sources of calories.
8. True. People who have had one heart attack are at much higher risk for a second attack. Reducing blood cholesterol levels can greatly slow down (and, in some people, even reverse) the buildup of cholesterol and fat in the wall of the coronary arteries and significantly reduce the chances of a second heart attack. If you have had a heart attack or have coronary heart disease, your LDL level should be around 100 mg/dL which is even lower than the recommended level of less than 130 mg/dL for the general population.

(Continued)

9. False. Children from high-risk families, in which a parent has high blood cholesterol (240 mg/dL or above) or in which a parent or grandparent has had heart disease at an early age (at 55 years or younger), should have their cholesterol levels tested. If a child from such a family has a cholesterol level that is high, it should be lowered under medical supervision, primarily with diet, to reduce the risk of developing heart disease as an adult. For most children, who are not from high-risk families, the best way to reduce the risk of adult heart disease is to follow a low saturated fat, low cholesterol eating pattern.

10. False. Blood cholesterol levels in both men and women begin to go up around age 20. Women before menopause have levels that are lower than men of the same age. After menopause, a woman's LDL-cholesterol level goes up—and so her risk for heart disease increases. For both men and women, heart disease is the number one cause of death.

11. True. Food labels have been changed. Look on the nutrition label for the amount of saturated fat, total fat, cholesterol, and total calories in a serving of the product. Use this information to compare similar products. Also, look for the list of ingredients. Here, the ingredient in the greatest amount is first and the ingredient in the least amount is last. So to choose food low in saturated fat or total fat, go easy on products that list fats or oil first, or that list many fat and oil ingredients.

Source: National Institutes of Health. www.nhlbi.nih.gov/health/public/heart or the online personal heart risk calculator at http://hin.nhlbi.nih.gov/atpiii/calculator.asp?usertype=pub.

Your Health Change Plan

for Lowering Heart Disease Risk

1. **Maintain a healthy weight**
   - Check with your health care provider to see if you need to lose weight.
   - If you do, lose weight slowly using a healthy eating plan and engaging in physical activity.
2. **Be physically active**
   - Engage in physical activity for a minimum of 30 minutes on most days of the week.
   - Combine everyday chores with moderate-level sporting activities, such as walking, to achieve your physical activity goals.
3. **Follow a healthy eating plan**
   - Set up a healthy eating plan with foods low in saturated fat, total fat, and cholesterol, and high in fruits, vegetables, and low fat dairy foods.
   - Write down everything that you eat and drink in a food diary. Note areas that are successful or need improvement.
   - If you are trying to lose weight, choose an eating plan that is lower in calories.
4. **Reduce sodium in your diet**
   - Choose foods that are low in salt and other forms of sodium.
   - Use spices, garlic, and onions to add flavor to your meals without adding more sodium.
5. **Drink alcohol only in moderation**
   - In addition to raising blood pressure, too much alcohol can add unneeded calories to your diet.
   - If you drink alcoholic beverages, have only a moderate amount—one drink a day for women, two drinks a day for men.
6. **Take prescribed drugs as directed**
   - If you need drugs to help lower your blood pressure or cholesterol, you still must follow the lifestyle changes mentioned above.
   - Use notes and other reminders to help you remember to take your drugs.

Source: NHLBI

Self Survey — Are You at Risk of Cancer?

Answer the following questions:

1. Do you protect your skin from overexposure to the sun? _____
2. Do you abstain from smoking or using tobacco in any form? _____
3. If you're over 40 or if family members have had colon cancer, do you get routine digital rectal exams? _____
4. Do you eat a balanced diet that includes the recommended Daily Value for vitamins A, B, and C? _____
5. If you're a woman, do you have regular Pap tests and pelvic exams? _____
6. If you're a man over 40, do you get regular prostate exams? _____
7. If you have burn scars or a history of chronic skin infections, do you get regular checkups? _____
8. Do you avoid smoked, salted, pickled, and high–nitrite foods? _____
9. If your job exposes you to asbestos, radiation, cadmium, or other environmental hazards, do you get regular checkups? _____
10. Do you limit your consumption of alcohol? _____
11. Do you avoid using tanning salons or home sunlamps? _____
12. If you're a woman, do you examine your breasts every month for lumps? _____
13. Do you eat plenty of vegetables and other sources of fiber? _____
14. If you're a man, do you perform regular testicular self-exams? _____
15. Do you wear protective sunglasses in sunlight? _____
16. Do you follow a low-fat diet? _____
17. Do you know the cancer warning signs? _____

Scoring:

If you answered no to any of the questions, your risk for developing various kinds of cancer may be increased.

Your Health Change Plan
for Early Detection of Cancer

Site	Recommendation	
Breast	Women 40 and older should have an annual mammogram, an annual clinical breast examination (CBE) by a health-care professional, and should perform monthly breast self-examinations (BSE). Ideally the CBE should occur before the scheduled mammogram. Women ages 20–39 should have a CBE by a health-care professional every 3 years and should perform BSE monthly.	 © Bill Crump/Brand X Pictures/PictureQuest
Colon and Rectum	Beginning at age 50 men and women should follow one of the examination schedules below: • A fecal occult blood test (FOBT) every year • A flexible sigmoidoscopy (FSIG) every 5 years • Annual fecal occult blood test and flexible sigmoidoscopy every five years* • A double-contrast barium enema every 5 years • A colonoscopy every 10 years* *Combined testing is preferred over either annual FOBT, or FSIG every 5 years, alone. People who are at moderate or high risk for colorectal cancer should talk with a doctor about a different testing schedule.	 © 2001 PhotoDisc, Inc.
Prostate	The PSA test and the digital rectal examination should be offered annually, beginning at age 50, to men who have a life expectancy of at least 10 years. Men at high risk (African American men and men with a strong family history of one or more first-degree relatives diagnosed with prostate cancer at an early age) should begin testing at age 45. For both men at average risk and high risk, information should be provided about what is known and what is uncertain about the benefits and limitations of early detection and treatment of prostate cancer so that they can make an informed decision about testing.	 © Corbis Images

(Continued)

Site	Recommendation
Uterus	**Cervix:** Screening should begin approximately three years after a woman begins having vaginal intercourse, but no later than 21 years of age. Screening should be done every year with regular Pap tests or every two years using liquid-based tests. At or after age 30, women who have had three normal test results in a row may get screened every 2–3 years. However, doctors may suggest a woman get screened more often if she has certain risk factors, such as HIV infection or a weak immune system. Women 70 years and older who have had three or more consecutive normal Pap tests in the last 10 years may choose to stop cervical cancer screening. Screening after total hysterectomy (with removal of the cervix) is not necessary unless the surgery was done as a treatment for cervical cancer.  **Endometrium:** The American Cancer Society recommends that all women should be informed about the risks and symptoms of endometrial cancer, and strongly encouraged to report any unexpected bleeding or spotting to their physicians. Annual screening for endometrial cancer with endometrial biopsy beginning at age 35 should be offered to women with or at risk for hereditary nonpolyposis colon cancer (HNPCC).
Cancer-related checkup	For individuals undergoing periodic health examinations, a cancer-related checkup should include health counseling, and depending on a person's age, might include examinations for cancers of the thyroid, oral cavity, skin, lymph nodes, testes, and ovaries, as well as for some nonmalignant diseases.

© 2001 PhotoDisc, Inc.

© Corbis Images

1. You want a second opinion, but your doctor dismisses your request for other physicians' names as unnecessary. Do you:
   a. Assume that he or she is right and you would merely be wasting time.
   b. Suspect that your physician has something to hide and immediately switch doctors.
   c. Contact your health plan and request a second opinion.

2. As soon as you enter your doctor's office, you get tongue-tied. When you try to find the words to describe what's wrong, your physician keeps interrupting. When giving advice, your doctor uses such technical language that you can't understand what it means. Do you:
   a. Prepare better for your next appointment.
   b. Pretend that you understand what your doctor is talking about.
   c. Decide you'd be better off with someone who specializes in complementary/alternative therapies and seems less intimidating.

3. You feel like you're running on empty, tired all the time, worn to the bone. A friend suggests some herbal supplements that promise to boost energy and restore vitality. Do you:
   a. Immediately start taking them.
   b. Say that you think herbs are for cooking.
   c. Find out as much as you can about the herbal compounds and ask your doctor if they're safe and effective.

4. Your hometown physician's office won't give you a copy of your medical records to take with you to college. Do you:
   a. Hope you won't need them and head off without your records.
   b. Threaten to sue.
   c. Politely ask the office administrator to tell you the particular law or statute that bars you from your records.

5. Your doctor has been treating you for an infection for three weeks, and you don't seem to be getting any better. Do you:
   a. Talk to your doctor, by phone or in person, and say, "This doesn't seem to be working. Is there anything else we can try?"
   b. Stop taking the antibiotic.
   c. Try an herbal remedy that your roommate recommends.

6. Your doctor suggests a cutting-edge treatment for your condition, but your health plan or HMO refuses to pay for it. Do you:
   a. Try to get a loan to cover the costs.
   b. Settle for whatever treatment options are covered.
   c. Challenge your health plan.

7. You call for an appointment with your doctor and are told nothing is available for four months. Do you:
   a. Take whatever time you can get whenever you can get it.
   b. Explain your condition to the nurse or receptionist, detailing any symptoms and pain you're experiencing.
   c. Give up and decide you don't need to see a doctor at all.

8. Even though you've been doing sit-ups faithfully, your waist still looks flabby. When you see an ad for waist-whittling liposuction, do you:
   a. Call for an appointment.
   b. Talk to a health-care professional about a total fitness program that may help you lose excess pounds.
   c. Carefully research the risks and costs of the procedure.

9. You have a condition that you do not want anyone to know about, including your health insurer and any potential employer. Do you:
   a. Use a false name.
   b. Give your physician a written request for confidentiality about this condition.
   c. Seek help outside the health-care system.

10. Your doctor suggests a biopsy of a funny-looking mole that's sprouted on your nose. Rather than using a laboratory that specializes in skin analysis, your HMO requires that all samples be sent to a general lab, where results may not be as precise. Do you:
   a. Ask your doctor to request that a specialty pathologist at the general lab perform the analysis.
   b. Hope that in your case, the general lab will do a good-enough job.
   c. Threaten to change HMOs.

Answers:
1: c; 2: a; 3: c; 4: c; 5: a; 6: c; 7: b; 8: b and c; 9: b; 10: a

Your Health Change Plan for

Protecting Yourself from Medical

Mistakes and Misdeeds

Just as physicians practice "defensive" medicine to protect themselves from legal liability, today's patients should take preventive steps to defend themselves from potentially harmful health services.

The Whats, Whys, and Hows of Medical Testing

:: Before undergoing any test, find out why you need it. Get a specific answer, not a "just in case" or "for your

(Continued)

peace of mind." If you've had the test before, could the earlier results be used? Would a follow-up exam be just as helpful?

:: Get some practical information as well: Should you do specific things before the test (such as not eat for a specified period)? How long will the test take? What will the test feel like? Will you need help getting home afterward?

:: Check out the risks. Any invasive test—one that penetrates the body with a needle, tube, or viewing instrument—involves some risk of infection, bleeding, or tissue damage. Tests involving radiation also present risks, and some people develop allergic reactions to the materials used in testing.

:: Get information on the laboratory that will be evaluating the test. Ask how often **false positives** or **false**

negatives occur. (False positives are abnormal results indicating that you have a particular condition when you really don't; false negatives indicate that you don't have a particular condition when you really do.) Find out about civil or criminal **negligence** suits filed against the laboratory on charges such as failing to diagnose cervical cancer because of incorrect reading of Pap smears.

:: You'll also want to know what happens when the test indicates a problem: Will the test be repeated? Will a different test be performed? Will treatment begin immediately? Could any medications you're taking (including nonprescription drugs, like aspirin) affect the testing procedures or results?

:: If you have a test, don't assume that no news is good news. Check back to get the results.

Answer true or false.

1. Everyone becomes "senile" sooner or later, if he or she lives long enough.
2. American families have by and large abandoned their older members.
3. Depression is a serious problem for older people.
4. The numbers of older people are growing.
5. The vast majority of older people are self-sufficient.
6. Mental confusion is an inevitable, incurable consequence of old age.
7. Intelligence declines with age.
8. Sexual urges and activity normally cease around age 55–60.
9. If a person has been smoking for 30 or 40 years, it does no good to quit.
10. Older people should stop exercising and rest.
11. As you grow older, you need more vitamins and minerals to stay healthy.
12. Only children need to be concerned about calcium for strong bones and teeth.
13. Extremes of heat and cold can be particularly dangerous to old people.
14. Many older people are hurt in accidents that could have been prevented.
15. More men than women survive to old age.
16. Death from stroke and heart disease are declining.
17. Older people on the average take more medications than younger people.
18. Snake oil salesmen are as common today as they were on the frontier.
19. Personality changes with age, just like hair color and skin texture.
20. Sight declines with age.

Scoring

1. False. Even among those who live to be 80 or older, only 20–25 percent develop Alzheimer's disease or some other incurable form of brain disease. "Senility" is a meaningless term that should be discarded.
2. False. The American family is still the number one caretaker of older Americans. Most older people live close to their children and see them often; many live with their spouses. In all, 8 out of 10 men and 6 out of 10 women live in family settings.
3. True. Depression, loss of self-esteem, loneliness, and anxiety can become more common as older people face retirement, the deaths of relatives and friends, and other such crises—often at the same time. Fortunately, depression is treatable.
4. True. Today, 12 percent of the U.S. population are 65 or older. By the year 2030, one in five people will be over 65 years of age.

5. True. Only 5 percent of the older population live in nursing homes; the rest are basically healthy and self-sufficient.
6. False. Mental confusion and serious forgetfulness in old age can be caused by Alzheimer's disease or other conditions that cause incurable damage to the brain, but some 100 other problems can cause the same symptoms. A minor head injury, a high fever, poor nutrition, adverse drug reactions, and depression can all be treated and the confusion will be cured.
7. False. Intelligence per se does not decline without reason. Most people maintain their intellect or improve as they grow older.
8. False. Most older people can lead an active, satisfying sex life.
9. False. Stopping smoking at any age not only reduces the risk of cancer and heart disease, it also leads to healthier lungs.
10. False. Many older people enjoy—and benefit from—exercises such as walking, swimming, and bicycle riding. Exercise at any age can help strengthen the heart and lungs, and lower blood pressure. See your physician before beginning a new exercise program.
11. False. Although certain requirements, such as that for "sunshine" vitamin D, may increase slightly with age, older people need the same amounts of most vitamins and minerals as younger people. Older people in particular should eat nutritious food and cut down on sweets, salty snack foods, high-calorie drinks, and alcohol.
12. False. Older people require fewer calories, but adequate intake of calcium for strong bones can become more important as you grow older. This is particularly true for women, whose risk of osteoporosis increases after menopause. Milk and cheese are rich in calcium as are cooked dried beans, collards, and broccoli. Some people need calcium supplements as well.
13. True. The body's thermostat tends to function less efficiently with age and the older person's body may be less able to adapt to heat or cold.
14. True. Falls are the most common cause of injuries among the elderly. Good safety habits, including proper lighting, nonskid carpets, and keeping living areas free of obstacles, can help prevent serious accidents.
15. False. Women tend to outlive men by an average of 8 years. There are 150 women for every 100 men over age 65, and nearly 250 women for every 100 men over 85.
16. True. Fewer men and women are dying of stroke or heart disease.
17. True. The elderly consume 25 percent of all medications and, as a result, have many more problems with adverse drug reactions.

(Continued)

18. True. Medical quackery is a $10 billion business in the United States. People of all ages are commonly duped into "quick cures" for aging, arthritis, and cancer.
19. False. Personality doesn't change with age. Therefore, all old people can't be described as rigid and cantankerous. You are what you are for as long as you live. But you can change what you do to help yourself to good health.

20. False. Although changes in vision become more co mon with age, any change in vision, regardless of ag related to a specific disease. If you are having proble with your vision, see your doctor.

Source: National Institute on Aging, www.counselingnotes.com/seniors/age/age_iq.h

Your Health Change Plan

for Preparing for a Medical Crisis

in an Aging Relative

"Medical crises are more common and more likely to lead to serious complications after age 60," says Kenneth Brummel-Smith, M.D., former president of the American Geriatrics Society. As your parents, grandparents, and other relatives get older, here is what you can do in advance:

:: ***Watch for warning signals.*** If your relative begins stumbling or having near-misses on the highway, make sure he or she sees a doctor before a serious fall or accident occurs. There may be a cure or, if not a cure, a way to improve functioning.

:: ***Suggest a surrogate.*** Even if a couple has been married for 40 years, neither has the legal right to make medical decisions for a spouse. The same is true for children and other relatives. The only way to get that right is to fill out a form, usually called an advance directive or legal power of attorney.

:: ***Talk to loved ones.*** "Waiting for something bad to happen doesn't make it any easier to talk about," says Dr. Brummel-Smith, who suggests sitting down for a formal discussion at some point after a relative reaches age 65 "but definitely before age 75."

:: ***Focus on values.*** "You don't have to discuss every possible drug or surgery or intervention," says Dr. Brummel-Smith. "What's important is that you under-

stand the older person's values. What are fates wors than death? Independence may be more important than living a longer life." Many families use the "Five Wishes" form (available online at www. agingwithdignity.org) to discuss preferences for med ical, personal, emotional, and spiritual care.

:: ***Involve the person's primary physician.*** Often it's no question of what doctors can do medically in a crisi but of what they should do, which is the patient's d sion. Encourage loved ones to discuss "what ifs" wit their doctors and make their desires clear. For instan a primary physician should know which treatments patients want (such as resuscitation during surgery) well as those they don't want (such as remaining on ventilator if unable to breathe on their own.)

:: ***Investigate alternative living options.*** Aging parents should visit retirement communities or nursing hom while they're still healthy, not with the idea of movi into them, but of knowing what's available. They als should find out if their health plan or HMO provid services for seniors after a medical crisis.

:: ***Make sure you know where to find key documents.*** A easily accessible folder with copies of the latest lab reports, consultations, and advance directives helps avoid unnecessary tests and get faster treatment whe crisis does occur.

DORMITORY SECURITY

YES	NO	STUDENTS:
____	____	Card swipe (like hotels)
____	____	Patented keys
____	____	Standard keys
____	____	Propped doors
____	____	Doors locked at night
____	____	Doors never locked
____	____	Doors always locked
____	____	Guards on duty (24 hrs.)

VISITORS:

____	____	Intercom at entrance
____	____	Show ID
____	____	Sign-in guests

DORM FEATURES:

____	____	Single sex dorms
____	____	Freshman dorms
____	____	Coed dorms
____	____	Senior dorms
____	____	Alcohol prohibited
____	____	Drugs prohibited
____	____	Substance-free
____	____	Propped door alarms
____	____	Fire sprinklers
____	____	Peep hole in room door
____	____	Dead bolt in room door
____	____	Safety chain on room door
____	____	Toilet in room
____	____	Shower in room
____	____	Bathrooms down hallway
____	____	Single sex bathrooms
____	____	Female hall bathrooms locked
____	____	Single sex floors locked
____	____	Secure windows (1st & 2nd floors)
____	____	Panic alarms in rooms

SECURITY PATROLS IN DORMS:

____	____	By police nightly
____	____	By security nightly
____	____	By students (unreliable)
____	____	By no one

**ROOMMATES QUICKLY
TRANSFERRED BY DEAN FOR:**

____	____	Using illegal drugs
____	____	Having sex
____	____	Underage drinking
____	____	Throwing up after drinking
____	____	Noisy parties
____	____	Hate speech
____	____	Physical abuse
____	____	You have to move out instead!!

CAMPUS SECURITY

YES	NO	CAMPUS SECURITY FORCE:
____	____	Sworn police
____	____	Arrest power
____	____	Patrolling day
____	____	Patrolling night
____	____	Carry fire arms
____	____	Security guards
____	____	Bicycle patrols
____	____	Surveillance cameras
____	____	Emergency phones
____	____	Student amateurs
____	____	Escort services
____	____	Shuttle services

HEALTH SERVICES:

____	____	Rape crisis center
____	____	Alcohol - drug counselors
____	____	AA meetings on campus

PARENTAL INVOLVEMENT

PARENTAL NOTIFICATION:

____	____	For underage drinkers
____	____	For alcohol poisoning
____	____	For illegal drug use
____	____	For acts of violence
____	____	For public drunkenness
____	____	For housing fire arms
____	____	For sexual assault
____	____	For hate crimes or speech
____	____	For academic probation
____	____	For disciplinary probation
____	____	For residence hall violations
____	____	For DUI convictions

CAMPUS JUDICIAL SYSTEM:

____	____	Open campus judicial hearings
____	____	Reveal names of campus sex offenders

Get campus crime statistics for the last 3 years from admissions office:

CRIMINAL OFFENSES

Murder	
Forcible sex offenses	____
Nonforcible sex offenses	____
Robbery	____
Aggravated assault	____
Burglary	____
Arson	____
Motor vehicle theft	____
Hate crimes	____
Total criminal offenses	____
Per student crime ratio	____

(Continued)

CAMPUS ARRESTS

Liquor law violations _____
Drug law violations _____
Weapons violations _____
TOTAL CAMPUS ARRESTS _____

Calculate campus crimes per thousand students and compare them with other schools. Also, attempt a balanced evaluation by combining your subjective impressions with any calculations.

Source: Security on Campus, Inc. www.securityoncampus.org

Your Health Change Plan
for Personal Safety on Campus

FUNDAMENTALS

- Freshmen should "respectfully decline" to have photo and personal information published for distribution to the campus community. Fraternities and upperclassmen have abused this type of publication to "target" naive freshmen.
- Study the campus and neighborhood with respect to routes between your residence and class/activities schedule. Know where emergency phones are located.
- Share your class/activities schedule with parents and a network of close friends, effectively creating a type of "buddy" system. Give network telephone numbers to your parents, advisors, and friends.
- Always travel in groups. Use a shuttle service after dark. Never walk alone at night. Avoid shortcuts.
- Survey the campus, academic buildings, residence halls, and other facilities while classes are in session and after dark to see that buildings, walkways, quadrangles, and parking lots are adequately secured, lit, and patrolled. Are emergency phones, escorts, and shuttle services adequate?
- To gauge the social scene, drive down fraternity row on weekend nights and stroll through the student hangouts. Are people behaving responsibly, or does the situation seem reckless and potentially dangerous? Remember, alcohol and/or drug abuse is involved in about 90 percent of campus crime. Carefully evaluate off-campus student apartment complexes and fraternity houses if you plan to live off-campus.

RESIDENCE

- Doors and windows to your residence hall should be equipped with quality locking mechanisms. Room doors should be equipped with peep holes and deadbolts.

Always lock them when you are absent. Do not loan out your key. Rekey locks when a key is lost or stolen.
- Card access systems are far superior to standard metal key and lock systems. Card access enables immediate lock changes when keys are lost, stolen, or when housing arrangements change. Most hotels and hospitals have changed to card access systems for safety reasons. Higher education institutions need to adopt similar safety features.
- Always lock your doors and 1st and 2nd floor windows at night. Never compromise your safety for a roommate who asks you to leave the door unlocked.
- Dormitories should have a central entrance/exit lobby where nighttime access is monitored, as well as an outside telephone which visitors must use to gain access.
- Dormitory residents should insist that residential assistants and security patrols routinely check for propped doors—day and night.
- Do not leave your identification, wallets, checkbooks, jewelry, cameras, and other valuables in open view.
- Program your phone's speed dial memory with emergency numbers that include family and friends.
- Know your neighbors and don't be reluctant to report illegal activities and suspicious loitering.

OFF-CAMPUS RESIDENTS

Off-campus residents should contact their student legal aid representative to draft leases that stipulate minimum standards of security and responsibility. Students and parents should also consult any "Neighborhood Watch" association active in the community or the municipal police regarding local crime rates.

Source: Reprinted with permission by Security on Campus, Inc. www.securityoncampus.org. Security on Campus assists victims of campus crime.

You may think that there is little you can do, as an individual, to save Earth. But everyday acts can add up and make a difference in helping or harming the planet on which we live.

	Almost Never	Sometimes	Always
1. Do you walk, cycle, carpool, or use public transportation as much as possible to get around?	_____	_____	_____
2. Do you recycle?	_____	_____	_____
3. Do you reuse plastic and paper bags?	_____	_____	_____
4. Do you try to conserve water by not running the tap as you shampoo or brush your teeth?	_____	_____	_____
5. Do you use products made of recycled materials?	_____	_____	_____
6. Do you drive a car that gets good fuel mileage and has up-to-date emission control equipment?	_____	_____	_____
7. Do you turn off lights, televisions, and appliances when you're not using them?	_____	_____	_____
8. Do you avoid buying products that are elaborately packaged?	_____	_____	_____
9. Do you use glass jars and waxed paper rather than plastic wrap for storing food?	_____	_____	_____
10. Do you take brief showers rather than baths?	_____	_____	_____
11. Do you use cloth towels and napkins rather than paper products?	_____	_____	_____
12. When listening to music, do you keep the volume low?	_____	_____	_____
13. Do you try to avoid any potential carcinogens, such as asbestos, mercury, or benzene?	_____	_____	_____
14. Are you careful to dispose of hazardous materials (such as automobile oil or antifreeze) at appropriate sites?	_____	_____	_____
15. Do you follow environmental issues in your community and write your state or federal representative to support "green" legislation?	_____	_____	_____

Count the number of items you've checked in each column. If you've circled 10 or more in the "always" column, you're definitely helping to make a difference. If you've circled 10 or more in the "never" column, read this chapter carefully and "Your Health Change Plan for Protecting the Planet" to find out what you can do. If you've mainly circled "sometimes," you're moving in the right direction, but you need to be more consistent and more conscientious.

Your Health Change Plan

for Protecting the Planet

By the choices you make and the actions you take, you can improve the state of the world. No one expects you to sacrifice every comfort or spend great amounts of money. However, for almost everyone, there's plenty of room for improvement. If enough people make small individual changes, they can have an enormous impact.

One basic environmental action is **precycling:** buying products packaged in recycled materials. According to Earthworks, a consumer group, packaging makes up a third of what people in the United States throw away. When you precycle, you consider how you're going to dispose of a product and the packaging materials before purchasing it. For example, you might choose eggs in recyclable cardboard packages rather than in plastic cartons, and look for juice and milk in refillable bottles.

Recycling—collecting, reprocessing, marketing, and using materials once considered trash—has become a necessity for several reasons: We've run out of space for all the garbage we produce; waste sites are often health and safety hazards; recycling is cheaper than landfill storage or incineration (a major source of air pollution); and recycling helps save energy and natural resources. Different communities take different approaches to recycling. Many provide regular curbside pickup of recyclables, which is so convenient that a majority of those eligible for such services participate. Most programs pick up bottles, cans, and newspapers—either separated or mixed together. Other communities have drop-off centers where consumers can leave recyclables. Conveniently located and sponsored by community organizations (such as charities or schools), these centers accept beverage containers, newspapers, cardboard, metals, and other items.

(Continued)

Buyback centers, usually run by private companies, pay for recyclables. Many centers specialize in aluminum cans, which offer the most profit. Some operate in supermarket parking lots; other centers have regular hours and staff members who carefully weigh and evaluate recyclables. In some places, reverse vending machines accept returned beverage containers and provide deposit refunds, in the form of either cash or vouchers.

Discarded computers and other electronic devices should also be recycled, by donating them to schools or charitable organizations. "Tech trash" buried in landfills is creating a new hazard because trace amounts of potentially hazardous agents, such as lead and mercury, can leak into the ground and water.

With *composting*—which some people describe as nature's way of recycling—the benefits can be seen as close as your backyard. Organic products, such as leftover food and vegetable peels, are mixed with straw or other dry material and kept damp. Bacteria eat the organic material and turn it into a rich soil. Some people keep a compost pile (which should be stirred every few days) in their backyard; others take their organic garbage (including mowed grass and dead leaves) to community gardens or municipal composting sites.

In *An Invitation to Health,* I emphasize that you shoulder a great deal of responsibility for your health and the quality of your life. Given the complexity of our minds and bodies and the many social and environmental factors that affect us, this responsibility can be a very heavy burden. But your load can be made lighter if you know where to turn for health information, services, and support.

In this directory, you will find more than 100 health-related topics and about 250 resources, including addresses, phone numbers, and websites for government agencies, community organizations, professional associations, recovery groups, and Internet sources. Many of these organizations and groups have toll-free 800 or 888 phone numbers, and most have websites (one caution: as you may have experienced, website addresses—like street addresses and phone numbers—change on occasion). Much of the material available from these groups is free.

Also included in Your Health Directory are clearinghouses and information centers that are especially rich sources of health knowledge. Their main purpose is to collect, help manage, and disseminate information. Clearinghouses often perform other services as well, such as creating original publications and providing tailored responses to individual requests. These organizations also may provide referrals to other groups that can help you.

Many of the groups listed here have local offices or chapters. You can call, write, or visit the websites of these organizations to find out if there is a branch in your vicinity, or you can check your local telephone directory.

The purpose of this directory is to help you be in control of your health. If you know where to turn for answers to your questions and if you know what choices you have, you may

find that you have more control over your life.

Resources by Topic

Abortion

National Abortion Federation
(provides information about abortion and referral for abortion services)
1755 Massachusetts Ave., N.W. Suite #600
Washington, DC 20036
(202) 667-5881
(800) 772-9100
www.prochoice.org

Accident Prevention

Centers for Disease Control and Prevention
1600 Clifton Rd. N.E.
Atlanta, GA 30333
(404) 639-3311
www.cdc.gov

National Safety Council
1121 Spring Lake Dr.
Itasca, IL 60143-3201
(630) 285-1121
(800) 621-7619
www.nsc.org

Adoption

AASK (Adopt a Special Kid)
(provides assistance to families who adopt older and handicapped children)
1025 N. Reynolds Rd.
Toledo, OH 43615
(800) 246-1731
(419) 534-3350
www.adoptamerica.org

Aging

Administration on Aging
U.S. Department of Health and Human Services
200 Independence Ave., S.W.
Washington, DC 20201
(800) 677-1116 (Eldercare Locator—to find services for an older person in his or her locality)
(202) 619-0724 (AoA's National Aging Information Center)
Fax: (202) 260-1012
E-mail: aoainfo@aoa.gov
www.aoa.gov

American Association of Retired Persons
601 E St., N.W.
Washington, DC 20049
(800) 424-3410
(202) 434-2277
www.aarp.org

Gray Panthers
733 15th St., N.W., Suite 437
Washington, DC 20005
(800) 280-5362
(202) 737-6637
www.graypanthers.org

AIDS (Acquired Immunodeficiency Syndrome)

National Center for HIV, STD, and TB Prevention (NCHSTP)

Centers for Disease Control and Prevention
1600 Clifton Rd. N.E.
Atlanta, GA 30333
(800) 311-3435
(404) 639-3311
www.cdc.gov/hiv/dhap.htm

University of California at San Francisco HIV Insite
4150 Clement St., Bldg. 16 VAMC 111V-UCSF
San Francisco, CA 94121
Fax: (415) 379-5547
E-mail: info@hivinsite.ucsf.edu
www.hivinsite.ucsf.edu

Gay Men's Health Crisis
119 West 24th St.
New York, NY 10011
(800) 243-7692
(212) 807-6664
www.gmhc.org

National AIDS Hotline
(800) 342-2437

San Francisco AIDS Foundation
995 Market St. #200
San Francisco, CA 94103
(415) 487-3000
www.sfaf.org

Alcohol Abuse and Alcoholism

Al-Anon and Alateen
(support groups for friends and relatives of alcoholics)
1600 Corporate Landing Pkwy.

Virginia Beach, VA 23454
(888) 425-2666
(757) 499-1443
www.al-anon-alateen.org
See also white pages of telephone directory for listing of local chapter

Alcohol Hotline
(800) ALCOHOL

Alcoholics Anonymous
475 Riverside Dr., 11th Floor
New York, NY 10115
(212) 647-1680
www.alcoholics-anonymous.org
See also white pages or telephone directory for listing of local chapter

National Association of Children of Alcoholics
11426 Rockville Pike, Suite 100
Rockville, MD 20852
(888) 554-COAS (554-2627)
(301) 468-0985
www.nacoa.org

National Clearinghouse for Alcohol and Drug Information
P.O. Box 2345
Rockville, MD 20847-2345
(800) 729-6686
(301) 468-2600
www.health.org/

National Institute on Alcohol Abuse and Alcoholism
6000 Executive Blvd.
Willco Building
Bethesda, MD 20892-7003
(301) 443-3860
www.niaaa.nih.gov
See also Drug Abuse; Drinking & Driving Groups

Allopathic Medicine

American Medical Association
515 N. State St.
Chicago, IL 60610
(312) 464-5000
www.ama-assn.org

Alternative Medicine

National Center for Complementary and Alternative Medicine (NCCAM)
P.O. Box 7923
Gaithersburg, MD 20898
(888) 644-6226
International: (301) 519-3153
TTY: (866) 464-3615 (toll-free)
www.nccam.nih.gov

Alzheimer's Disease

Alzheimer's Association National Office
919 N. Michigan Ave., Suite 1000

Chicago, IL 60611-1676
(800) 272-3900
(312) 335-8700
www.alz.org

Arthritis

Arthritis Foundation
1330 West Peachtree St.
Atlanta, GA 30309
(800) 283-7800
(404) 872-7100
www.arthritis.org

National Institute of Arthritis and Musculoskeletal and Skin Diseases
National Institutes of Health
1 Ams Circle
Bethesda, MD 20892-3675
(301) 495-4484
(877) 22-NIAMS (226-4267)
E-mail: NIAMSInfo@mail.nih.gov
www.nih.gov/niams

Asthma

Asthma and Allergy Foundation of America
1233 20th St., N.W., Suite 402
Washington, DC 20036
(800) 7-ASTHMA (727-8462)
(202) 466-7643
Fax: (202) 466-8940
www.aafa.org

Lung Line
National Jewish Medical Research Center
(information and referral service)
1400 Jackson St.
Denver, CO 80206
(800) 222-5864
(303) 388-4461
www.njc.org

Attention Deficit Disorder

National Attention Deficit Disorder Association (National ADDA)
1788 Second St., Suite 200
Highland Park, IL 60035
(847) 432-ADDA
www.add.org

Children and Adults with Attention Deficit Disorder (CHADD)
8181 Professional Place, Suite 201
Landover, MD 20785
(800) 233-4050
(301) 306-7070
www.chadd.org/

Automobile Safety

American Automobile Association (AAA)
1000 AAA Dr. #28
Heathrow, FL 32746-5080
(407) 444-4240

www.aaa.com
See also white or yellow pages of telephone directory for listing of local chapter

Insurance Institute for Highway Safety
1005 North Glebe Rd., Suite 800
Arlington, VA 22201
(703) 247-1500
www.highwaysafety.org/

National Highway Traffic Safety Administration
Office of Publications
400 7th St., S.W.
Washington, DC 20590
(888) 327-4236
(202) 366-0123
www.nhtsa.dot.gov

Auto Safety Hotline
(for consumer complaints about auto safety and child safety seats, and requests for information on recalls)
(800) 424-9393

Birth Control and Family Planning

Advocates for Youth
(develops programs and material to educate youth on sex and sexual responsibility)
1025 Vermont Ave. N.W., Suite 200
Washington, DC 20005
(202) 347-5700
Fax: (202) 347-2263
E-mail: info@advocatesforyouth.org
www.advocatesforyouth.org

American College of Obstetricians and Gynecologists
(provides literature and contraceptive information)
409 12th Street, S.W.
P.O. Box 96920
Washington, DC 20090-6920
(202) 638-5577
www.acog.com

Engender Health
(provides information and referrals to individuals considering tubal ligation or vasectomy)
440 Ninth Ave.
New York, NY 10001
(212) 561-8000
www.engenderhealth.org

Planned Parenthood Federation of America (PPFA)
434 West 33rd St.
New York, NY 10001
(212) 541-7800
www.plannedparenthood.org
See also white or yellow pages of telephone directory for listing of local chapter

Birth Defects

Cystic Fibrosis Foundation (CFF)
6931 Arlington Rd.
Bethesda, MD 20814
(800) FIGHT-CF (344-4823)
(301) 951-4422
Fax: (301) 951-6378
www.cff.org

March of Dimes Birth Defects Foundation
1275 Mamaroneck Ave.
White Plains, NY 10605
(888) 663-4637
(914) 428-7100
www.modimes.org

Blindness

American Foundation for the Blind
11 Penn Plaza, Suite 300
New York, NY 10001
(800) AFB-LINE (232-5463)
(212) 502-7600
www.afb.org

National Federation of the Blind
1800 Johnson St.
Baltimore, MD 21230
(800) 638-7518
(410) 659-9314
www.nfb.org

National Library Service for the Blind and Physically Handicapped
Library of Congress
1291 Taylor St., N.W.
Washington, DC 20011
(800) 424-8567
(202) 707-5100
www.loc.gov/nls

Blood Banks

American Red Cross
431 18th St., N.W.
Washington, DC 20006
(202) 639-3520
www.redcross.org
See also white or yellow pages of telephone directory for listing of local chapter

Breast Cancer

Reach to Recovery
(support program for women who have undergone mastectomies as a result of breast cancer)
American Cancer Society
2200 Lake Blvd.
Atlanta, GA 30319
(800) 227-2345
(404) 816-7800
www.cancer.org

Cancer

American Cancer Society
American Cancer Society
2200 Lake Blvd.
Atlanta, GA 30319
(800) 227-2345
(404) 816-7800
www.cancer.org

Cancer Information Service
National Cancer Institute
Suite 3036A
6116 Executive Blvd.
Bethesda, MD 20892
(800) 4-CANCER (422-6237)
(301) 435-3848
www.cis.nci.nih.gov/

Leukemia & Lymphoma Society of America
1311 Mamaroneck Ave.
White Plains, NY 10605
(914) 949-5213
Fax: (914) 949-6691
www.leukemia.org

National Coalition for Cancer Survivorship
1010 Wayne Ave., Suite 770
Silver Spring, MD 20910-5600
(301) 650-9127
(877) NCCS-YES (622-7937)
Fax: (301) 565-9670
www.canceradvocacy.org

R. A. Bloch Cancer Foundation (Cancer Connection)
(support group that matches cancer patients with volunteers who are cured, in remission, or being treated for same type of cancer)
4400 Main St.
Kansas City, MO 64111
(800) 433-0464
(816) 932-8453
www.blochcancer.org

Child Abuse

National Child Assault Prevention
(provides services to children, adolescents, mentally retarded adults, and elderly)
606 Delsea Drive
Sewell, NJ 08080
(800) 258-3189
www.ncap.org

National Child Abuse Hotline
(800) 422-4453

National Committee for the Prevention of Child Abuse
(provides literature on child abuse prevention programs)
200 S. Michigan Ave., 17th Floor
Chicago, IL 60604-2404
(312) 663-3520
www.preventchildabuse.org

Parents Anonymous
(self-help group for abusive parents)
675 W. Foothill Blvd., Suite 220
Claremont, CA 91711-3475
(909) 621-6184
Fax: (909) 625-6304
www.parentsanonymous.org

Childbirth

American College of Nurse-Midwives
(R.N.s who provide services through the maternity cycle)
818 Connecticut Ave., N.W.
Suite 900
Washington, DC 20006
(202) 728-9860
www.midwife.org

American College of Obstetricians and Gynecologists
409 12th St., S.W.
P.O. Box 96920
Washington, DC 20090-6920
(202) 638-5577
www.acog.com

Lamaze International
2025 M St., Suite 800
Washington, DC 20036-3309
(800) 368-4404
(202) 367-1128
Fax: (202) 367-2128
www.lamaze-childbirth.com

International Childbirth Education Association
P.O. Box 20048
Minneapolis, MN 55420
(952) 854-8660
Fax: (952) 854-8772
www.icea.org

Child Health and Development

National Center for Education in Maternal and Child Health
Georgetown University
Box 571272
Washington, DC 20007-2292
(202) 784-9770
Fax: (202) 784-9777
www.ncemch.org

National Institute of Child Health & Human Development
Bldg. 31, Rm. 2A32, MSC 2425
31 Center Dr.
Bethesda, MD 20892-2425
(800) 370-2943
www.nichd.nih.gov

Chiropractic

American Chiropractic Association
1701 Clarendon Blvd.
Arlington, VA 22209

(800) 986-4632
Fax: (703) 243-2593
www.amerchiro.org

Consumer Information

Federal Consumer Information Center
(catalog of publications developed by federal agencies for consumers)
Department WWW
Pueblo, CO 81009
(888) 878-3256
www.pueblo.gsa.gov

U.S. Consumer Product Safety Commission
Office of Information Services
4330 East-West Highway
Bethesda, MD 20814-4408
(800) 638-2772
(301) 504-6816
Fax: (301) 504-0124 and (301) 504-0025
E-mail: info@cpsc.gov
www.cpsc.gov

Consumers Union of United States
(tests quality and safety of consumer products: publishes *Consumer Reports* magazine)
101 Truman Ave.
Yonkers, NY 10703
(914) 378-2000
www.consumerreports.org

Council of Better Business Bureaus
4200 Wilson Blvd., Suite 800
Arlington, VA 22203-1804
(703) 276-0100
Fax: (703) 525-8277
www.bbb.org
See also white or yellow pages of telephone directory for listing of local chapter

Food and Drug Administration (FDA)
Office of Consumer Affairs
Consumer Inquiries
5600 Fishers Lane
Rockville, MD 20857
(888) INFO-FDA (463-6332)
www.fda.gov

Crime Victims

Crisis Prevention Institute, Inc.
(offers programs on nonviolent physical crisis interventions)
3315-K North 124th St.
Brookfield, WI 53005
(800) 558-8976 (U.S. and Canada)
(262) 783-5787
www.crisisprevention.com

National Center for Victims of Crime
2000 M Street, N.W., Suite 480
Washington, DC 20010

(202) 467-8700
Fax: (202) 467-8701
www.ncvc.org

Death and Grieving

Share
(support group for parents who have lost a newborn)
c/o St. Joseph's Health Center
300 First Capitol Dr.
St. Charles, MO 63301-2893
(800) 821-6819
(636) 947-6164
www.nationalshareoffice.com

Dental Health

American Dental Association (ADA)
211 E. Chicago Ave.
Chicago, IL 60611
(312) 440-2500
www.ada.org

National Institute of Dental Research
Public Information & Liaison Branch
45 Center Dr., MSC 6400
Bethesda, MD 20892-6400
(301) 496-4261
www.nidr.nih.gov

Depressive Disorders

American Psychiatric Association
1000 Wilson Blvd., Suite 1825
Arlington, VA 22209-3901
(888) 357-7924
(703) 907-7300
E-mail: apa@psych.org
www.psych.org

American Psychological Association
750 First St., N.E.
Washington, DC 20002-4242
(800) 374-2721
(202) 336-5510
TDD/TTY: (202) 336-6123
www.apa.org

Depression & Bipolar Support Alliance
730 N. Franklin, Suite 501
Chicago, IL 60610-7204
(800) 826-3632
(312) 642-0049
Fax: (312) 642-7243
www.dbsalliance.org

DES (Diethylstibestrol)

DES Action, USA
(support group for persons exposed to DES)
610 16th St., Suite 301
Oakland, CA 94612
(510) 465-4011
Fax: (510) 465-4815
www.desaction.org

Diabetes

American Diabetes Association
National Center
1701 North Beauregard St.
Alexandria, VA 22311
(800) DIABETES (342-2383)
(703) 549-1500
www.diabetes.org

Juvenile Diabetes Research Foundation International (JDRFI)
120 Wall St.
New York, NY 10005-4001
(800) JDF-CURE (533-2873)
(212) 785-9500
Fax: (212) 785-9595
www.jdfcure.org

National Diabetes Information Clearinghouse
1 Information Way
Bethesda, MD 20892-3560
(800) 860-8747
(301) 654-3327
E-mail: ndic@info.niddk.nih.gov
www.niddk.nih.gov/health/diabetes/ndic.htm

Digestive Diseases

National Institute of Diabetes & Digestive & Kidney Diseases (NIDDK)
Office of Communication & Public Liaison
NIDDK, NIH, Building 31
Room 9A04 Center Dr., MSC 2560
Bethesda, MD 20892-2560
(301) 654-3810
www.niddk.nih.gov

Disabled Services

American Alliance for Health, Physical Education, Recreation & Dance (AAHPERD)
(provides information about recreation and fitness opportunities for the disabled)
1900 Association Drive
Reston, VA 20191-1598
(800) 213-7193
Fax: (703) 476-9527
www.aahperd.org

National Library Service for the Blind and Physically Handicapped
Library of Congress
1291 Taylor St., N.W.
Washington, DC 20011
(800) 424-8567
(202) 707-5100
TDD: (202) 707-0744
Fax: (202) 707-0712
www.loc.gov/nls

Special Olympics International (SOI)
1325 G St., N.W.
Suite 500
Washington, DC 20005
(202) 628-3630
Fax: (202) 824-0200
www.specialolympics.org

Domestic Violence

National Coalition Against Domestic Violence (NCADV)
P.O. Box 18749
Denver, CO 80218
(303) 839-1852
Fax: (303) 831-9851
www.ncadv.org

National Domestic Violence Hotline
(800) 799-SAFE (799-7233)

National Network to End Domestic Violence
660 Pennsylvania, SE, Suite 303
Washington, DC 20003
(202) 543-5566
www.nnedv.org

Down Syndrome

National Association for Down Syndrome (NADS)
P.O. Box 4542
Oak Brook, IL 60522-4542
(630) 325-9112
www.nads.org

National Down Syndrome Society
666 Broadway, 8th Floor
New York, NY 10012-2317
(800) 221-4602
(212) 460-9330
www.ndss.org

Drug Abuse

Cocaine Anonymous World Services
P.O. Box 2000
Los Angeles, CA 90049-8000 or
3740 Overland Ave., Ste. C
Los Angeles, CA 90034
(800) 347-8998
(310) 559-5833
www.ca.org

Narcotics Anonymous (NA)
(support group for recovering narcotics
    addicts)
P.O. Box 9999
Van Nuys, CA 91409
(818) 773-9999
Fax: (818) 700-0700
www.na.org
See also white or yellow pages of tele-
    phone directory for local chapter

National Cocaine Hotline
(800) COCAINE (262-2463)

National Institute on Drug Abuse
6001 Executive Blvd., Room 5213
Bethesda, MD 20892-9651
(301) 443-1124
Helpline: (800) 662-4357
www.nida.nih.gov

National Parents Resource Institute for Drug Education (PRIDE)
166 St. Charles St.
Bowling Green, KY 42101
(800) 279-6361
Fax: (270) 746-9598
www.prideusa.org

Center for Substance Abuse Prevention (CSAP)
Substance Abuse and Mental Health
    Administration
5600 Fishers Lane
Rockwall 2 Bldg.
Rockville, MD 20857
(301) 443-8956
www.prevention.samhsa.gov

Drinking and Driving Groups

Mothers Against Drunk Driving
511 E. John Carpenter Frwy., Suite 700
Irving, TX 75062
(800) GET-MADD (438-6233)
(214) 744-6233
www.madd.org
See also white or yellow pages of telephone directory for local chapter

Students Against Destructive Decisions (also Students Against Driving Drunk (SADD))
Box 800
Marlboro, MA 01752
(877) SADD-INC (723-3462)
(508) 481-3568
Fax: (508) 481-5759
www.saddonline.com

Eating Disorders

National Eating Disorders Association (NEDA)
(self-help groups that provide information
    and referrals to physicians and therapists)
603 Stewart St., Suite 803
Seattle, WA 98101
(800) 931-2237
(206) 382-3587
www.nationaleatingdisorders.org

Anorexia Nervosa and Related Eating Disorders (ANRED)
(provides information and referrals for
    people with eating disorders)
P.O. Box 5102
Eugene, OR 97405
(541) 344-1144
www.anred.com

Environment

U.S. Environmental Protection Agency (EPA)
Ariel Rios Bldg.
1200 Pennsylvania Ave., N.W.
Washington, DC 20460
(202) 260-2090
www.epa.gov

Greenpeace, USA
702 H St. N.W.
Washington, DC 20001
(800) 326-0959
(202) 462-1177
www.greenpeaceusa.org

Natural Resources Defense Council
40 West 20th St.
New York, NY 10011
(212) 727-2700
Fax: (212) 727-1773
www.nrdc.org

Sierra Club
85 2nd St., 2nd Floor
San Francisco, CA 94105-3441
(415) 977-5500
(415) 977-5799
www.sierraclub.org

World Wildlife Fund
1250 24th St., N.W.
P.O. Box 97180
Washington, DC 20090-7180
(800) CALL-WWF (225-5993)
(202) 293-4800
Fax: (202) 293-2911
www.wwfus.org

Epilepsy

Epilepsy Foundation of America
4351 Garden City Drive
Landover, MD 20785-7223
(800) EFA-1000 (332-1000)
(301) 459-3700
www.efa.org

Gay and Lesbian Organizations and Services

Human Rights Campaign
919 18th St., N.W., Suite 800
Washington, DC 20006
(202) 628-4160
Fax: (202) 347-5323
www.hrc.org

National Gay and Lesbian Task Force (NGLTF)
1325 Massachusetts Ave., N.W., Suite 600
Washington, DC, 20005
(202) 393-5177
Fax: (202) 393-2241
www.ngltf.org

Parents, Families, and Friends of Lesbians and Gays (PFLAG)
1726 M St., N.W., Suite 400
Washington, DC 20036
(202) 467-8180
Fax: (202) 467-8194
www.pflag.org

Genetics

American College of Medical Genetics
9650 Rockville Pike
Bethesda, MD 20814-3998
(301) 634-7127
Fax: (301) 571-0677
E-mail: acmg@faseb.org
www.acmg.net

The Human Genome Organization
HUGO Americas
Laboratory of Genetics
National Institute on Aging
NIH/NIA-IRP. GRC, Box 31
5600 Nathan Shock Dr.
Baltimore, MD 21224-6825
(410) 558-8337
Fax: (410) 558-8331
E-mail: schlessingerd@grc.nia.nih.gov

GeneTests—GeneClinics
(a database of information for patients and families with genetic disorders, providing access to support groups)
University of Washington School of Medicine
Seattle, WA
www.genetests.org

Hazardous Waste

Environmental Protection Agency (EPA)
Ariel Rios Bldg.
1200 Pennsylvania Ave., N.W.
Washington, DC 20460
(202) 260-2090
www.epa.gov

Hazardous Waste Hotline Information
(800) 424-9346

Health Care

Association for Applied and Therapeutic Humor (AATH)
(publishes a newsletter and sponsors seminars for people in the helping professions)
1951 W. Camelback Rd., Suite 445
Phoenix, AZ 85015
(602) 995-1454
FAX: (602) 995-1449
www.aath.org

American Medical Association
515 N. State St.
Chicago, IL 60610
(312) 464-5000
www.ama-assn.org

American Nurses Association
600 Maryland Ave., S.W.
Suite 100 West
Washington, DC 20024-2571
(800) 274-4ANA (274-4262)
(202) 651-7000
www.ana.org

Health Education

National Center for Chronic Disease Prevention and Health Promotion
Centers for Disease Control and Prevention
Mail Stop A34
1600 Clifton Rd., N.E.
Atlanta, GA 30333
(404) 639-3534
(800) 311-3435
www.cdc.gov/nccdphp

Hearing Impairment

American Society for Deaf Children
(resource group for parents of hard of hearing and deaf children)
P.O. Box 3355
Gettysburg, PA 17325
(717) 334-7922
Fax: (717) 334-8808
(800) 942-ASDC (Parent Hotline)
www.deafchildren.org

Better Hearing Institute (BHI)
(provides educational and resource materials on deafness)
Better Hearing Institute
515 King St., Suite 420
Alexandria, VA 22314
(703) 684-3391
www.betterhearing.org

Heart Disease

American Heart Association (AHA)
7272 Greenville Ave.
Dallas, TX 75231
(800) 242-8721
(214) 373-6300
www.americanheart.org

National Heart, Lung, and Blood Institute
(provides information on cardiovascular risk factors and disease)
Bldg. 31, Room 5A52
31 Center Dr., MSC 2486
Bethesda, MD 20892
(800) 575-9355
(301) 592-8573
www.nhlbi.nih.gov/index.htm

Helping Others

United Way of America
701 N. Fairfax St.
Alexandria, VA 22314-2045
(703) 836-7100
www.unitedway.org

Hospice

The National Hospice and Palliative Care Organization
1700 Diagonal Rd., Suite 625
Alexandria, VA 22314
(703) 837-1500
(800) 646-6460
www.nhpco.org

Immunization

National Immunization Program
Centers for Disease Control
Mail Stop E-05
1600 Clifton Rd., N.E.
Atlanta, GA 30333
(404) 639-3311
(800) 232-2522
www.cdc.gov/nip/diseases/adult-vpd.htm

Immunization Action Coalition
(information for children, adolescents, and adults)
1573 Selby Ave., Suite 234
St. Paul, MN 55104
(651) 647-9009
Fax: (651) 647-9131
www.immunize.org

Infant Care

La Leche League International
(provides information and support to women interested in breast-feeding)
1400 N. Meacham Rd.
Schaumburg, IL 60168-4079
(800) LA-LECHE (525-3243)
(847) 519-7730
www.lalecheleague.org

Infectious Diseases

Centers for Disease Control and Prevention
1600 Clifton Rd., N.E.
Atlanta, GA 30333
(800) 311-3435
(404) 639-3534
www.cdc.gov

Infertility

Resolve: The National Infertility Association
(offers counseling, information, and support to people with problems of infertility)

1310 Broadway
Somerville, MA 02144-1779
(888) 623-0744
(617) 623-0744
www.resolve.org

Kidney Disease

American Kidney Fund (AKF)
(provides information on financial aid to
patients, organ transplants, and kidney-
related diseases)
6110 Executive Blvd., Suite 1010
Rockville, MD 20852
(800) 638-8299
(301) 881-3052
www.akfinc.org

American Association of Kidney Patients (AAKP)
3505 E. Frontage Rd., Suite 315
Tampa, FL 33607
(800) 749-2257
Fax: (813) 636-8122
www.aakp.org

National Kidney Foundation (NKF)
30 East 33rd St., Suite 1100
New York, NY 10016
(800) 622-9010
(212) 889-2210
Fax: (212) 689-9261
www.kidney.org

Liver Disease

American Liver Foundation (ALF)
75 Maiden, Suite 603
New York, NY 10038
(800) 465-4837
(212) 668-1000
www.liverfoundation.org/

Lung Disease

American Lung Association
61 Broadway, 6th Floor
New York, NY 10006
(212) 315-8700
www.lungusa.org

National Heart, Lung, and Blood Institute
(provides information on cardiovascular
risk factors and disease)
Bldg. 31, Room 5A52
31 Center Dr., MSC 2486
Bethesda, MD 20892
(800) 575-9355
www.nhlbi.nih.gov/index.htm

Lupus Erythematosus

Lupus Foundation of America (LPA)
1300 Piccard Dr., Suite 200
Rockville, MD 20850-4303
(301) 670-9292

(800) 558-0121
www.lupus.org/lupus/index.html

Marriage and Family

Women Work! The National Network for Women's Employment
(national advocacy group for women over
35 who have lost their primary means
of support through death, divorce, or
disabling of spouse)
1625 K St. N.W., Suite 300
Washington, DC 20006
(202) 467-6346
www.womenwork.org

Alliance for Children & Families
11700 West Lake Park Dr.
Milwaukee, WI 53224-3099
(414) 359-1040
Fax: (414) 359-1074
E-mail: info@alliance1.org
www.alliance1.org

Stepfamily Association of America
(provides information and publishes quar-
terly newsletter)
650 J St., Suite 205
Lincoln, NE 68508
(800) 735-0329
(402) 477-7837
Fax: (402) 477-8317
www.stepfam.org

Medications

(Prescriptions and Over-the-Counter)

Food and Drug Administration (FDA)
Office of Consumer Affairs Public
Inquiries
5600 Fishers Lane (HFE-88)
Rockville, MD 20857-0001
(888) 463-6332 (INFO-FDA)
www.fda.gov

Mental Health

American Psychiatric Association
1000 Wilson Blvd., Suite 125
Arlington, VA 22209
(888) 357-7924
(703) 907-7300
E-mail: apa@psych.org
www.psych.org

American Psychological Association
750 First St., N.E.
Washington, DC 20002-4242
(800) 374-2721
(202) 336-5510
TDD/TTY: (202) 336-6123
www.apa.org

American Psychoanalytic Foundation
9 Breakers Isle
Dana Point, CA 92629

(503) 244-5700
E-mail: APF@cyberpsych.org
www.cyberpsych.org/apf

National Alliance for the Mentally Ill (NAMI)
(self-help advocacy organization for persons with schizophrenia and depressive
disorders and their families)
Colonial Place Three
2107 Wilson Blvd., Suite 300
Arlington, VA 22201
(703) 524-7600
HelpLine: (800) 950-NAMI (950-6264)
www.nami.org/

National Institute of Mental Health
Information Resources and Inquiries
Branch
6001 Executive Blvd., Room 8184
MSC 9663
Bethesda, MD 20892-9663
(301) 443-4513
Fax: (301) 443-4279
TTY: (301) 443-8431
E-mail: nimhinfo@nih.gov
www.nimh.nih.gov/

National Mental Health Association (NMHA)
2001 N. Beauregard St., 12 Floor
Alexandria, VA 22311
(800) 969-NMHA (969-6642)
(703) 684-7722
Fax: (703) 684-5968
www.nmha.org

Mental Retardation

Association for Retarded Citizens (ARC)
1010 Wayne Ave., Suite 650
Silver Spring, MD 20910
(301) 565-3842
E-mail: info@thearc.org
www.thearc.org

Missing and Runaway Children

Child Find of America
(800) I-AM-LOST (426-5678)
Runaway Hotline
(800) 621-4000
www.childfindofamerica.org

National Center for Missing and Exploited Children (NCMEC)
699 Prince St., Suite 550
Alexandria, VA 22314
(703) 274-3900
Fax: (703) 274-2200
24-hour Hotline:
(800) THE-LOST (843-5678)
www.missingkids.org

Neurological Disorders

National Institute of Neurological Disorders and Stroke
National Institutes of Health
31 Center Dr., Room 8A18
Bethesda, MD 20892-2540
(800) 352-9424
(301) 496-5751
Fax: (301) 402-2186
E-mail: braininfo@ninds.nih.gov
www.ninds.nih.gov

Nutrition

American Dietetic Association
120 South Riverside Plaza, Suite 2000
Chicago, IL 60606-6995
(312) 899-0040
www.eatright.org

American Society for Nutritional Sciences
9650 Rockville Pike, Suite 4500
Bethesda, MD 20814-3990
(301) 530-7050
Fax: (301) 571-1892
www.asns.org

Food and Drug Administration (FDA)
Office of Consumer Affairs
Public Inquiries
5600 Fishers Lane (HFE-88)
Rockville, MD 20857
(888) 463-6332 (INFO-FDA)
www.fda.gov

Food and Nutrition Information Center
U.S. Dept. of Agriculture
National Agricultural Library
10301 Baltimore Ave.
Beltsville, MD 20705-2351
(301) 504-5719
Fax: (301) 504-6409
TTY: (301) 504-6856
E-mail:fnic@nal.usda.gov
www.nal.usda.gov/fnic

Center for Nutrition in Sport and Human Performance
206A Chenoweth Lab
University of Massachusetts
Amherst, MA 01002
(413) 545-1076
Fax: (413) 545-1074
E-mail: volpe@nutrition.umass.edu
www.umass.edu/cnshp/

National Dairy Council
10255 W. Higgins Rd., Suite 900
Rosemont, IL 60018-5616
(800) 426-8271
www.nationaldairycouncil.org

Occupational Safety and Health

Occupational Safety and Health Administration (OSHA)
U.S. Dept. of Labor
Office of Public Affairs, Room N3647
200 Constitution Ave.
Washington, DC 20210
(202) 693-1999
(800) 321-OSHA (6742)
TTY: (877) 889-5627
www.osha.gov

Organ Donations

The Living Bank (TLB)
(provides information and acts as registry and referral service for people wanting to donate organs for research or transplantation)
P.O. Box 6725
Houston, TX 77265
(800) 528-2971
www.livingbank.org

Osteopathic Medicine

American Osteopathic Association (AOA)
142 East Ontario St.
Chicago, IL 60611
(800) 621-1773
(312) 202-8000
Fax: (312) 202-8200
E-mail: info@aoa-net.org
www.aoa-net.org

Parent Support Groups

National Organization of Mothers of Twins Clubs (NOMOTC)
P.O. Box 438
Thompson Station, TN 37179-0438
(877) 540-2200
(615) 595-0936
www.nomotc.org

Parents Anonymous
(self-help group for abusive parents)
675 W. Foothill Blvd., Suite 220
Claremont, CA 91711-3475
(909) 621-6184
Fax: (909) 625-6304
E-mail: parentsanonymous@
    parentsanonymous.org
www.parentsanonymous.org

Parents Without Partners, Inc.
1650 South Dixie Highway, Suite 510
Boca Raton, FL 33432
(561) 391-8833
Fax: (561) 395-8557
E-mail: pwp@jti.net
www.parentswithoutpartners.org

Parenting

National Parent Information Network
ERIC Clearinghouse on Elementary and Early Childhood Education
University of Illinois at Urbana-Champaign
Children's Research Center
51 Gerty Dr.
Champaign, IL 61820-7469
(800) 583-4135
(217) 333-1386
Fax: (217) 333-3767
www.npin.org

Phobias

Anxiety Disorders Association of America (ADAA)
(provides information about phobias and referrals to therapists and support groups)
8730 Georgia Ave., Suite 600
Silver Spring, MD 20910
(240) 485-1001
Fax: (240) 485-1035
www.adaa.org

TERRAP Programs
(headquarters for national network of treatment clinics for agoraphobia)
932 Evelyn St.
Menlo Park, CA 94025
(415) 327-1312
(800) 2-PHOBIA (274-6242)
www.terrap.com

Physical Fitness

See local yellow and white pages of telephone directory for listing of local health clubs and YMCAs, YWCAs, and Jewish Community Centers

Cooper Institutes for Aerobics Research
12330 Preston Rd.
Dallas, TX 75230
(972) 341-3200
Fax: (972) 341-3227
E-mail: courses@cooperinst.org
www.cooperinst.org

President's Council on Physical Fitness and Sports
Dept. W 200 Independence Ave., S.W.
Room 738 H
Washington, DC 20201
(202) 690-9000
Fax: (202) 690-5211
www.fitness.gov

American College of Sports Medicine
ACSM National Center
P.O. Box 1440

Indianapolis, IN 46206-1440
(317) 637-9200
www.acsm.org

Center for Nutrition in Sport and Human Performance
206A Chenoweth Lab
University of Massachusetts
Amherst, MA 01002
(413) 545-1076
Fax: (413) 545-1074
E-mail: volpe@nutrition.umass.edu
www.umass.edu/cnshp/

Poisoning

See emergency numbers listed in the front of your local phone directory

National Poison Hotline
(800) 962-1253

Pregnancy

National Institute of Child Health & Human Development
Bldg. 31, Room 2A32, MSC 2425
31 Center Dr.
Bethesda, MD 20892-2425
(800) 370-2943
www.nichd.nih.gov

Product Safety

U.S. Consumer Product Safety Commission
4330 East-West Highway
Bethesda, MD 20814-4408
(800) 638-CPSC (638-2772)
(301) 504-6816
www.cpsc.gov

Radiation Control and Safety

Center for Devices and Radiological Health

U.S. Food and Drug Administration
Office of Consumer Affairs
1350 Piccard Drive, HFZ-210
Rockville, MD 20850
(888) 463-6332
(301) 827-3990
www.fda.gov/cdrh/index.html

National Institute of Environmental Health Sciences

National Institutes of Health
P.O. Box 12233
Research Triangle Park, NC 27709
(919) 541-3345
www.niehs.nih.gov

Rape, Victimization

See white pages of telephone directory for listing of local rape crisis and counseling centers

National Center for Victims of Crime
2000 M St., N.W., Suite 480
Washington, DC 20010
(202) 467-8700
Fax: (202) 467-8701
www.ncvc.org

National Coalition Against Sexual Assault
125 N. Enola Dr.
Enola, PA 17025
(717) 728-9764
Fax: (717) 728-9781
www.dreamingdesigns.com/other/indexncasa.html

National Organization for Victim Assistance (NOVA)
1730 Park Rd. N.W.
Washington, DC 20010
(800) TRY-NOVA (879-6682)
(202) 232-6682
Fax: (202) 462-2255
www.try-nova.org

National Sexual Violence Resource Center
123 North Enola Dr.
Enola, PA 17025
(877) 739-3895
(717) 909-0710
Fax: (717) 909-0714
TTY: (717) 909-0715
E-mail: resources@nsvrc.org
www.nsvrc.org

Reye's Syndrome

National Reye's Syndrome Foundation
P.O. Box 829
Bryan, OH 43506-0829
(800) 233-7393 (U.S. only)
(419) 636-2679
Fax: (419) 636-9897
E-mail: nrsf@reyessyndrome.org
www.reyessyndrome.org

Self-Care/Self-Help

National Self-Help Clearinghouse (NSHC)
(provides information about self-help groups)
365 5th Ave., Suite 3300
New York, NY 10016
(212) 817-1822
http://selfhelpweb.org

Sex Education

American Association of Sex Educators, Counselors and Therapists (AASECT)
P.O. Box 5488
Richmond, VA 23220-0488

E-mail: AASECT@mediaone.net
www.aasect.org

Advocates for Youth
(develops programs and material to educate youth on sex and sexual responsibility)
1025 Vermont Ave. N.W., Suite 200
Washington, DC 20005
(202) 347-5700
Fax: (202) 347-2263
E-mail: info@advocatesforyouth.org
www.advocatesforyouth.org

Planned Parenthood Federation of America (PPFA)
434 West 33rd St.
New York, NY 10001
(212) 541-7800
www.plannedparenthood.org

Sexuality Information and Education Council of the U.S. (SIECUS)
(maintains an information clearinghouse on all aspects of human sexuality)
130 West 42nd St., Suite 350
New York, NY 10036-7802
(212) 819-9770
Fax: (212) 819-9776
E-mail: siecus@siecus.org
www.siecus.org

Sexual Abuse and Assault

National Center for Assault Prevention
(provides services to children, adolescents, mentally retarded adults, and elderly)
606 Delsea Dr.
Sewell, NJ 08080
(800) 258-3189
(908) 369-8972
www.ncap.org/aboutncap.htm

Prevent Child Abuse America
200 S. Michigan Ave., Suite 1700
Chicago, IL 60604
(312) 663-3520
Fax: (312) 939-8962
www.preventchildabuse.org

Sexually Transmitted Infections

Centers for Disease Control and Prevention
1600 Clifton Rd. N.E.
Atlanta, GA 30333
(404) 639-3311
www.cdc.gov

American Social Health Association
P.O. Box 13827
Research Triangle Park, NC 27709
(919) 361-8400
Fax: (919) 361-8425
www.ashastd.org

National Herpes Resource Center
American Social Health Association
P.O. Box 13827
Research Triangle Park, NC 27709-3827
(919) 361-8488
www.ashastd.org/hrc/index.html

National STD Hotline
(800) 227-8922

Sexuality Information and Education Council of the U.S. (SIECUS)
(maintains an information clearinghouse on all aspects of human sexuality)
130 West 42nd St., Suite 350
New York, NY 10036-7802
(212) 819-9770
Fax: (212) 819-9776
E-mail: siecus@siecus.org
www.siecus.org

Sickle-Cell Disease

Sickle Cell Disease Association of America
200 Corporate Pointe, Suite 495
Culver City, CA 90230-7633
(800) 421-8453
(310) 216-6363
www.sicklecelldisease.org

The Sickle Cell Information Center
The Georgia Comprehensive Sickle Cell Center at Grady Health System
P.O. Box 109, Grady Memorial Hospital, 80 Jesse Hill Jr. Dr.
Atlanta, GA 30303
(404) 616-3572
Fax: (404) 616-5998
E-mail: aplatt@emory.edu
www.emory.edu/peds/sickle

Skin Diseases

American Academy of Dermatology
P.O. Box 4014
Schaumburg, IL 60168-4014
(888) 462-DERM (3376)
(847) 330-0230
Fax: (847) 330-0050
www.aad.org

University of Iowa Hospitals and Clinics

Department of Dermatology
200 Hawkins Drive BT 2045-1
Iowa City, IA 52242-1090
(319) 356-7500 (appointments only)
(319) 356-2274 (business only)
Fax: (319) 356-8317 (business only)
www.tray.dermatology.uiowa.edu

National Psoriasis Foundation
6600 SW 92nd Ave., Suite 300
Portland, OR 97223-7195
(800) 723-9166
(503) 244-7404
Fax: (503) 245-0626
getinfo@npfusa.org
www.psoriasis.org

Sleep and Sleep Disorders

American Sleep Apnea Association
1424 K St., N.W., Suite 302
Washington, DC 20005
(202) 293-3650
Fax: (202) 293-3656
E-mail: asaa@sleepapnea.org
www.sleepapnea.org

American Academy of Sleep Medicine
One Westbrook Corporate Center, Suite 920
West Chester, IL 60154
(708) 492-0930
Fax: (708) 492-0943
www.aasmnet.org

Better Sleep Council
501 Wythe St.
Alexandria, VA 22314
(703) 683-8371
www.bettersleep.org/

National Sleep Foundation
1522 K St., N.W., Suite 500
Washington, DC 20005
(202) 347-3471
Fax: (202) 347-3472
www.sleepfoundation.org

Smoking and Tobacco

Action on Smoking and Health (ASH)
(provides information on nonsmokers' rights and related subjects)
2013 H St., N.W.
Washington, DC 20006
(202) 659-4310
http://ash.org

American Cancer Society
(provides information about quitting smoking and smoking cessation programs)
2200 Lake Blvd.
Atlanta, GA 30319
(800) 227-2345
(404) 816-7800
www.cancer.org

American Heart Association
(provides information about quitting smoking and smoking cessation programs)
7272 Greenville Ave.
Dallas, TX 75231
(800) 242-8721
(214) 373-6300
www.americanheart.org

American Lung Association
(provides information about quitting smoking and smoking cessation programs)
61 Broadway, 6th Floor
New York, NY 10006
(212) 315-8700
To reach your local American Lung Association: (800) LUNG-USA (586-4872)
www.lungusa.org

Americans for Nonsmokers' Rights
2530 San Pablo Ave., Suite J
Berkeley, CA 94702
(510) 841-3032
Fax: (510) 841-3060
E-mail: anr@no-smoke.org
www.no-smoke.org

Stress Reduction

American Institute of Stress
124 Park Ave.
Yonkers, NY 10703
(914) 963-1200
Fax: (914) 965-6267
E-mail: stress124@earthlink.net
www.stress.org

American Psychological Association
750 First St., N.E.
Washington, DC 20002-4242
(800) 374-2721
(202) 336-5510
TDD/TTY: 202-336-6123
www.apa.org

Association for Applied Psychophysiology and Biofeedback
10200 W. 44th Ave., Suite 304
Wheat Ridge, CO 80033
www.aapb.org

Stroke

Council on Stroke
American Heart Association
7272 Greenville Ave.
Dallas, TX 75231
(214) 373-6300
www.americanheart.org

National Institute of Neurological Disorders and Stroke
National Institutes of Health
P.O. Box 5801
Bethesda, MD 20824
(800) 352-9424
(301) 496-5751
www.ninds.nih.gov/

Stuttering

National Center for Stuttering
200 East 33rd St.
New York, NY 10016

Hotline: (800) 221-2483
(212) 532-1460
www.stuttering.com

Sudden Infant Death Syndrome (SIDS)

SIDS Alliance
(provides information and referrals to families who have lost an infant because of SIDS)
1314 Bedford Ave., Suite 210
Baltimore, MD 21208
(800) 221-7437
(410) 653-8226
Fax: (410) 653-8709
E-mail: info@sidsalliance.org
www.sidsalliance.org

Suicide Prevention

American Association of Suicidology (AAS)
4201 Connecticut Ave., N.W., Suite 408
Washington, DC 20008
(202) 237-2280
National Hopeline: (800) SUICIDE
Fax: (202) 237-2282
E-mail: ajkulp@suicidology.org
www.suicidology.org

American Psychoanalytic Foundation
9 Breakers Isle
Dana Point, CA 92629
(503) 244-5700
www.cyberpsych.org/apf

Terminal Illness

Make-A-Wish Foundation of America (MAWFA)
(dedicated to granting the special wishes of terminally ill children)
3550 North Central Ave., Suite 300
Phoenix, AZ 85012-2127
(800) 722-WISH (722-9474)
(602) 279-WISH (279-9474)
Fax: (602) 279-0855
E-mail: mawfa@wish.org
www.wish.org

Make Today Count (MTC)
(self-help group for persons with terminal illness)
St. Johns Hospital
1235 E. Cherokee St.
Springfield, MO 65804
(800) 432-2273
(417) 885-3324

Victimization

National Center for Victims of Crime
2000 M St., N.W., Suite 480
Washington, DC 20036

(202) 467-8700
Fax: (202) 467-8701
www.ncvc.org

National Coalition Against Domestic Violence
P.O. Box 18749
Denver, CO 80218
(303) 839-1852
Fax: (303) 831-9251
www.ncadv.org

National Coalition Against Sexual Assault
125 N. Enola Dr.
Enola, PA 17025
(717) 728-9764
Fax: (717) 728-9781
http://dreamingdesigns.com/other/indexncasa.html

National Organization for Victim Assistance (NOVA)
1730 Park Rd., N.W.
Washington, DC 20010
(800) Try-NOVA (879-6682)
(202) 232-6682
Fax: (202) 462-2255
www.try-nova.org

Weight Control

Overeaters Anonymous (OA)
P.O. Box 44020
Rio Rancho, NM 87174-4020
(505) 891-2664
Fax: (505) 891-2664
E-mail: info@overeatersanonymous.org
www.oa.org

Weight-Control Information Network (WIN)
National Institute of Diabetes and Digestive and Kidney Diseases
1 WIN Way
Bethesda, MD 20892-3665
(877) 946-4627
(202) 828-1025
Fax: (202) 828-1028
E-mail: win@info.niddk.nih.gov
www.niddk.nih.gov/health/nutrit/win.htm

Take Off Pounds Sensibly (TOPS)
P.O. Box 07360
4575 S. Fifth St.
Milwaukee, WI 53207-0360
(800) 932-8677
(414) 482-4620
www.tops.org

Weight Watchers International
175 Crossways Park West
Woodbury, NY 11797
(516) 390-1657
www.weight-watchers.com

Wellness

National Wellness Institute, Inc.
1300 College Court
P.O. Box 827
Stevens Point, WI 54481-0827
(800) 243-8694
(715) 342-2969
Fax: (715) 342-2979
E-mail: nwi@nationalwellness.org
www.nationalwellness.org

Wellness Associates of Chicago
(publishes *The Wellness Inventory*)
4250 Marine Dr., Suite 200
Chicago, IL 60613
(773) 935-6377
Fax: (773) 929-4446
E-mail: info@wellnessofchicago.com
www.wellness-associates.com

Women's Health

National Women's Health Network (NWHN)
514 10th St., N.W., Suite 400
Washington, DC 20004
(202) 347-1140
Health Info: (202) 628-7814
Fax: (202) 347-1168
www.womenshealthnetwork.org

National Women's Health Information Center

U.S. Public Health Service on Women's Health
8550 Arlington Blvd., Suite 300
Fairfax, VA 22031
(800) 994-WOMAN (994-9662)
www.4women.gov

GenneX Healthcare Technologies, Inc.

Estronaut: A Forum for Women's Health
GenneX Healthcare Technologies, Inc.
207 E. Ohio, 186
Chicago, IL 60611
(312) 335-0095
E-mail: ask@gennexhealth.com
www.estronaut.com

Planned Parenthood
434 West 33rd St.
New York, NY 10001
(212) 541-7800
Fax: (212) 245-1845
www.plannedparenthood.org
See also white or yellow pages of telephone directory for listing of local chapter

By definition, an emergency is a situation in which you have to think and act fast. Start by assessing the circumstances. Shout for help if you're in a public place. Look for any possible dangers to you or the victim, such as a live electrical wire or a fire. Seek medical assistance as quickly as possible. Dial 911 or a local emergency phone number. Don't attempt rescue techniques, such as cardiopulmonary resuscitation (CPR), unless you are trained. If you have a car, be sure you know the shortest route from your home to the nearest 24-hour hospital emergency department.

✖ Supplies

Every home should have a kit of basic first aid supplies kept in a convenient location out of the reach of children. Stock it with the following:

- Bandages and sterile gauze pads
- Adhesive tape
- Scissors
- Cotton balls or absorbent cotton
- Cotton swabs
- Thermometer
- Antibiotic ointment
- Sharp needle
- Safety pins
- Calamine lotion

Keep a similar kit in your car or boat. You might want to add some extra items from your home, such as a flashlight, soap, blanket, paper cups, and any special equipment that a family member with a chronic illness may need.

✖ Bleeding

Blood loss is frightening and dangerous. Direct pressure stops external bleeding. Since internal bleeding can also be life-threatening, you must be aware of the warning signs.

For an Open Wound

1. Apply direct pressure over the site of the wound. Cover the entire wound.
2. Use sterile gauze, a sanitary napkin, a clean towel, sheet, or handkerchief or, if necessary, your washed bare hand. Ice or cold water in a pad will help stop bleeding and decrease swelling.
3. Apply firm, steady pressure for five to fifteen minutes. Most wounds stop bleeding within a few minutes.
4. If the wound is on a foot, hand, leg, or arm, use gravity to help slow the flow of blood. Elevate the limb so that it is higher than the victim's heart.
5. If the bleeding doesn't stop, press harder.
6. Seek medical attention if the bleeding was caused by a serious injury, if stitches will be needed to keep the wound closed, or if the victim has not had a tetanus booster within the last ten years.

For Internal Bleeding

1. Suspect internal bleeding if a person coughs up blood, vomits red or brown material that looks like coffee grounds, passes blood in urine or stool, or has black, tarlike bowel movements.
2. Do not let the victim take any medication or fluids by mouth until seen by a doctor, because surgery may be necessary.
3. Have the victim lie flat. Cover him or her lightly.
4. Seek immediate medical attention.

For a Bloody Nose

1. Have the victim sit down, leaning slightly forward so the blood does not run down his or her throat. The person should spit out any blood in his or her mouth.
2. Use the thumb and forefingers to pinch the nose. If the victim can do the pinching, apply a cold compress to the nose and surrounding area.
3. Apply pressure for ten minutes without interruption.
4. If pinching does not work, gently pack the nostril with gauze or a clean strip of cloth. Do not use absorbent cotton, which will stick. Let the ends hang out so you can remove the packing easily later. Pinch the nose, with the packing in place, for five minutes.
5. If a foreign object is in the nose, do not attempt to remove it. Ask the person to blow gently. If that does not work, seek medical attention.
6. The nose should not be blown or irritated for several hours after a nosebleed stops.

Breathing Problems

If a person appears to be unconscious, approach carefully. The victim may be in contact with electrical current. If so, make sure the electricity is shut off before touching the victim. The first function you should check is respiration. Tap or shake the victim's shoulder gently, shouting, "Are you all right?" Look for any signs of breathing: Can you hear breath sounds? Can you feel breath on your cheek? If the person is breathing, do not perform mouth-to-mouth resuscitation.

If you aren't certain if the victim is breathing, or if there are no signs of breath, follow these steps:

1. Lay the person on his or her back on the floor or ground. Roll the victim over if necessary, being careful to turn the head with the remainder of the body as a unit to avoid possible neck injury. Loosen any tight clothing around the neck or chest.
2. Check for any foreign material in the mouth or throat and remove it quickly.
3. Open the airway by tilting the head back and lifting the chin up.
4. Pinch the nostrils shut with your thumb and index finger.
5. Take a deep breath, open your mouth wide and place it securely over the victim's, and give two slow breaths, each lasting 1 to 10 seconds. Remove your mouth, turn your head, and check to see if the victim's chest rises and falls. If you hear air escaping from the victim's mouth and see the chest fall, you know that you are getting air into the lungs.
6. Repeat once every five seconds (twelve breaths per minute) until professional help takes over, or the victim begins breathing on his or her own. It may take several hours to revive someone. If you stop, the victim may not be able to breathe on his or her own. Once the person does begin to breathe independently, always get professional help.
7. If air doesn't seem to be entering the chest, or the chest doesn't fall between breaths, tilt the head further back. If that doesn't work, follow the directions for choking emergencies later in this section.
8. If the victim is a child, do not pinch the nose shut. Cover both the mouth and nose with your mouth, and place your free hand very lightly on the child's chest. Use small puffs of air rather than big breaths. Feel the chest inflate as you blow, and listen for exhaled air. Repeat once every three seconds (twenty breaths per minute).

Broken Bones

If you suspect that a person has broken a leg, do not move him or her unless there is immediate danger.

1. Check for signs of breathing. If there is none or breathing is very weak, administer mouth-to-mouth resuscitation.
2. If the person is bleeding, apply direct pressure on the site of the wound.
3. Try to keep the victim warm and calm.
4. Do not try to push a broken bone back into place if it is sticking out of the skin. You can apply a moist dressing to prevent it from drying out.
5. Do not try to straighten out a fracture.
6. Do not allow the victim to walk.
7. Splint unstable fractures to prevent painful motion.

Burns

1. If fire caused the burn, cool the affected area with water to stop the burning process.
2. Remove the victim's garments and jewelry and cover him or her with clean sheets or towels.
3. Call for help immediately.
4. If chemicals caused the burn, wash the affected area with cool water for at least 20 minutes. Chemical burns of the eye require immediate medical attention after flushing with water for 20 minutes.

Choking

A person with anything stuck in the throat and blocking the airway can stop breathing, lose consciousness, and die within four to six minutes. A universal signal of distress because of choking is clasping the throat with one or both hands. Other signs are an inability to talk and noisy, difficult breathing. You need to take immediate action, but NEVER slap the victim's back. This could make the obstruction worse.

If the victim can speak, cough, or breathe, do not interfere. Coughing alone may dislodge the foreign object. If the choking continues without lessening, call for medical help.

If the victim cannot speak, cough, or breathe but is conscious, use the Heimlich maneuver, as follows

1. Stand behind the victim (who may be seated or standing) and wrap your arms around his or her waist.
2. Make a fist with one hand and place the thumb side of your fist against the victim's abdomen, just above the navel. Grasp your fist with your other hand and press into his or her abdomen with a quick, upward thrust.

Do not exert any pressure against the rib cage with your forearms.

3. Repeat this procedure until the victim is no longer choking or loses consciousness.

4. If the person is lying face down, roll the victim over. Facing the person, kneel with your legs astride his or her hips. Put the heel of one hand below the rib cage and place your other hand on top. Press into the abdomen with a quick, upward thrust. Repeat thrusts as needed.

5. If you start choking when you're by yourself, place your fist below your rib cage and above your navel. Grasp this fist with your other hand and press into your abdomen with a quick, upward thrust. You also can lean over a fixed, horizontal object, such as a table edge or chair back, and press your upper abdomen against it with a quick, upward thrust. Repeat as needed until you dislodge the object.

If the Victim Is Unconscious

1. Place him or her on the ground and give mouth-to-mouth resuscitation as described earlier.

2. If the victim does not start breathing and air does not seem to be going into his or her lungs, roll the victim onto his or her back and give one or more manual thrusts: Place one of your hands on top of the other with the heel of the bottom hand in the middle of the abdomen, slightly above the navel and below the rib cage. Press into the abdomen with a quick, upward thrust. Do not push to either side. Repeat six to ten times as needed.

3. Clear the airway. Hold the victim's mouth open with one hand and use your thumb to depress the tongue. Make a hook with the index finger of your other hand and, using a gentle, sweeping motion, reach into the victim's throat and feel for a swallowed foreign object in the airway.

4. Repeat the following steps in this sequence:
   • Six to ten abdominal thrusts
   • Probe in mouth
   • Try to inflate lungs
   • Repeat

5. If the victim suddenly seems okay, but no foreign material has been removed, take him or her directly to the hospital. A foreign object, such as a fish or chicken bone or other jagged object, could do internal damage as it passes through the victim's system.

If the Victim Is a Child

1. If the child is coughing, do nothing. The coughing alone may dislodge the object.

2. If the airway is blocked and the child is panicky and fighting for breath, do *NOT* probe the airway with your fingers to clear an unseen foreign object. You might push the material back into the airway, worsening the obstruction.

3. For an infant younger than a year, hang the child over your arm so that the head is lower than the trunk. Using the heel of your hand, administer four firm blows high on the back between the shoulder blades. For a bigger child, follow the same procedure, but invert the child over your knee rather than your arm.

4. After four back blows, perform four chest thrusts (the Heimlich maneuver as described above).

✖ Drowning

A person can die of drowning four to six minutes after breathing stops. Although prevention is the wisest course, follow these steps in case of a drowning emergency:

1. Get the victim out of the water fast. Be extremely cautious, because a drowning person may panic and grasp at a rescuer, endangering that individual as well. If possible, push a branch or pole within the victim's reach.

2. If the victim is unconscious, use a flotation device if at all possible. Carefully place the person on the device. Once out of the water, place the victim on his or her back.

3. If the victim is not breathing, start mouth-to-mouth resuscitation. Continue until the person can breathe unassisted or help arrives. (Note that it may take an hour or two for a drowning victim to resume independent breathing.) Do not leave the victim alone for any reason.

4. Once the person is breathing without assistance, even if he or she is still coughing, you need only stay nearby until professional help arrives.

✖ Electrical Shock

1. If you suspect that an electrical shock has knocked a person unconscious, approach very carefully. Do not touch the victim unless the electricity has been turned off.

2. Shut off the power at the plug, circuit breaker, or fuse box. Simply shutting off an appliance does not remove the shock hazard. Use a dry stick to move a wire or downed power line from the victim. Keep in mind that you also are in danger until the power is off.

3. If the person's breathing is weak or has stopped, follow the steps for mouth-to-mouth resuscitation.

4. Even if the victim returns to consciousness, call for medical help. While waiting, cover the victim with a blanket or coat to keep him or her warm. Place a blanket underneath the body if the surface is cold. Be sure the person lies flat if conscious, with legs raised. If the

victim is unconscious, place him or her on one side, with a pillow supporting the head. Do not give the victim anything to eat or drink.

5. Electrical burns can extend deep into the tissue, even when they appear minor. Do not put butter, household remedies, or sprays on burns without a doctor's instruction. Do not use ice or cold water on an electrical burn that is more than 2 inches across.

Heart Attack

Chest pain can be caused by indigestion, strained muscles, or lung infections. The warning signs of a heart attack are:

- Intense pain that lasts for more than two minutes, produces a tight or crushing feeling, is centered in the chest, or spreads to the neck, jaw, shoulder, or arm
- Shortness of breath that is worse when the person lies flat and improves when the person sits
- Heavy sweating
- Nausea or vomiting
- Irregular pulse
- Pale or bluish skin or lips
- Weakness
- Severe anxiety, feeling of doom

If an individual develops these symptoms:

1. Call for emergency medical help immediately.
2. Have the person sit up or lie in a semi-reclining position. Loosen tight clothing. Keep him or her comfortably warm.
3. If the person loses consciousness, turn on his or her back and check for breathing and pulse. If vomiting occurs, turn the victim's head to one side and clean the mouth.
4. If the person has medicine for angina pectoris (chest pain) and is conscious, help him or her take it.
5. If the person is unconscious, and you are trained to perform cardiopulmonary resuscitation (CPR), check for a pulse at the wrist or neck. If there is none, beginCPR in conjunction with mouth-to-mouth resuscitation. Do not attempt CPR unless you are trained. It is not a technique you can learn from a book.

Poisoning

Many common household substances, including glue, aspirin, bleaches, and paint, can be poisonous. If you think someone has been poisoned, call the National Poison Control Center: (800) 222-1222. Be prepared to provide the following information:

- The kind of substance swallowed and how much was swallowed
- If a child or adult swallowed the substance
- Symptoms
- Whether or not vomiting has occurred
- Whether you gave the person anything to drink
- How much time it will take to get to an emergency room

The Poison Control Center will tell you whether or not to induce vomiting or neutralize a swallowed poison. Here are some additional guidelines:

1. Always assume the worst if a small child has swallowed or might have swallowed something poisonous. Keep the suspected item or container with you to answer questions.
2. Do not give any medications unless a physician or the Poison Control Center instructs you to do so.
3. Do not follow the directions for neutralizing poisons on the container unless a doctor or the Poison Control Center confirms that they are appropriate measures to take.
4. If the child is conscious, give moderate doses of water to dilute the poison.
5. If a poisoning victim is unconscious, make sure he or she is breathing. If not, give mouth-to-mouth resuscitation. Do not give anything by mouth or attempt to stimulate the person. Call for emergency help immediately.
6. If the person is vomiting, make sure he or she is in a position in which he or she cannot choke on what is brought up.
7. While vomiting is the fastest way to expel swallowed poisons from the body, never try to induce vomiting if the person has swallowed any acid or alkaline substance, which can cause burns of the face, mouth, and throat (examples include ammonia, bleach, dishwasher detergent, drain and toilet cleaners, lye, oven cleaners, or rust removers), or petroleum-like products, which produce dangerous fumes that can be inhaled during vomiting (examples include floor polish, furniture wax, gasoline, kerosene, lighter fluid, turpentine, and paint thinner).

✔ **What They Tell the Doctor**
✔ **How Often You Need Them**
✔ **What to Do About Abnormal Results**

Do you wonder what the doctor sees when he looks into your eyes with that little light or what it means when your blood or urine test is normal? In this section we cover some of the most common tests your doctor does, what they tell, and how often they should be done.

General Information

- Always ask your doctor what tests are being done, why they are being ordered, what they involve, and what the results mean.
- No test is foolproof. If a result is unexpected, whether normal or abnormal, your doctor should repeat the test before making any decisions.
- Modern X-ray machines expose you to a minuscule amount of radiation. Nevertheless, be sure to tell the physician or X-ray technician if there is even a chance you may be pregnant.
- Often a doctor orders a test because that is the only way to prove you do not have a disease.

Allergy Skin Testing

- Skin testing is still the most reliable method.
- The physician either pricks your skin 20 to 40 or more times to introduce a tiny bit of potentially allergic material or injects a small amount.
- Children who are frightened by multiple needle sticks and are unlikely to sit still for as long as necessary may have blood (RAST) tests instead.

What the results mean

If you develop redness or a hivelike bump around an area, you are probably allergic to the injected substance. Sometimes you can avoid the offending material, but things like pollen and dust are everywhere. Your allergist may recommend desensitizing shots to reduce your reac-

tion. The results of skin tests won't be reliable if you take antihistamines within 48 hours of the test.

How often to be tested

Skin tests are necessary only if you cannot get allergy relief from other measures such as over-the-counter medications, reducing mold and dust in the house, and staying away from animals.

Blood Pressure Reading

- High blood pressure, a major cause of stroke and heart attacks, usually causes no symptoms.
- The upper number in a reading—the systolic—refers to peak amount of pressure generated when your heart pumps blood, the lower number—the diastolic—measures the least amount of pressure.

What the results mean

Most doctors today think the lower the pressure the better, which means a reading of 120/80 or less. Because the mere anxiety of having your blood pressure taken can cause a mild elevation, your doctor will want to repeat an abnormal test, ideally on a different day, before diagnosing high blood pressure.

How often to be tested

Everyone—no matter how healthy—should have a blood-pressure reading taken at least once a year, more often if you have high blood pressure.

Blood Tests

- Blood may be taken from either a finger prick or, more commonly, a vein in your arm.
- See below for information on cholesterol testing, which is also done from a blood sample.

Complete Blood Count (CBC)

This is the most commonly performed of all blood tests.

What the results mean

A low red-cell count, called anemia, can be caused by something as simple as too little iron in your diet, as complex as an abnormality in your digestion, or as serious as a bone marrow problem or silent bleeding. Iron deficiency is the most frequent cause, with women who menstruate and limit their intake of red meat at the greatest risk. If your doctor diagnoses this problem, ask about making dietary changes as well as taking iron supplements.

A high white-cell count, a measure of the body's defenses against infection, usually indicates some kind of infection. Depending on the type of cell that predominates, your doctor may be able to identify whether you have a bacterial or viral infection.

Platelets, the first participants in blood clotting, may be decreased because of a viral infection, abnormal bleeding, or for no identifiable reason.

Chemistry Panels (Chem 12 or 18, SMA 12 or 24)

Kidney, bone, liver, pancreas, prostate, and some glandular functions are screened by these tests.

What the results mean

An abnormality may signal a problem that needs treatment. Because accuracy decreases when many tests are run together, any specific abnormal test should be repeated, especially if unexpected.

✖ CAT (Computerized Axial Tomography) Scan

- A CAT scan is 100 times more sensitive than an X ray.
- You lie as motionless as possible in a large tube while an X-ray beam travels 360 degrees around you. The test takes about an hour.

What the results mean

The test can help diagnose such conditions as tumors, blood clots, cysts, and bleeding in the brain as well as in various other organs.

✖ Cholesterol Test/ Lipoprotein Profile

- Anyone can have a high cholesterol level, but you are more apt to be at risk if there is a family history of early heart attacks, strokes, or high blood cholesterol.
- Your doctor will look at total blood cholesterol, high-density lipoprotein (HDL, the "good" cholesterol that prevents cholesterol from sticking to your blood vessels), low-density lipoprotein (LDL, the "bad" cholesterol that does the reverse), and triglycerides.

What the results mean

Experts today think optimum total cholesterol levels are below 200 mg/dL of blood. Persistently high cholesterol values will prompt your doctor to advise dietary and lifestyle changes—less fat intake, more exercise—and perhaps medication. Optimal LDL levels are less than 100 mg/dL, and optimal HDL levels are 60 mg/dL or higher.

How often to be tested

If your cholesterol level is under 200 and your LDL level is under 130, repeat the test every five years. If your test is borderline, repeat it annually. (Note that the test should be taken when you have not eaten for at least twelve hours.)

If you have a family history of cholesterol problems, have your children tested annually from age 2; if you don't, have them tested around age 10 and every few years thereafter. Children under 2 should not be given a low-cholesterol diet; they need extra fat to make brain tissue and hormones for growth.

✖ Fundoscopy

The doctor looks into your eye with a little light.

What the results mean

The beginnings of cataracts may be visible, as well as irregularities in the blood vessels that indicate damage from high cholesterol (fatty deposits in the blood vessels), high blood pressure (narrowing and notching), diabetes, or other diseases. If the optic nerve is swollen, there may be excess pressure inside your skull.

What your doctor *cannot* see are the early signs of glaucoma, which can lead to blindness if not treated. Over age 20, have a pressure check for glaucoma from an ophthalmologist or optometrist every three years—or every year if you have a family history of glaucoma.

✖ Heart Tests

- The following tests are listed from the simplest through the most complicated.
- Also see listings for blood pressure readings, cholesterol tests, and pulse.

Electrocardiogram (ECG, EKG)

A machine amplifies the electrical signals from your heart and records them on paper.

What the results mean

An EKG can detect such things as an enlarged heart, abnormal levels of potassium or calcium, disease of the small vessels of the heart, or the source of an abnormal heart rhythm. It is a nonspecific test, however, and more advanced studies should be done if serious disease is suspected.

Echocardiogram

In this painless test sound waves are used to produce a picture of the heart in action on a TV-type screen.

What the results mean

The test investigates the size of the heart chambers, the thickness of the walls, how the four heart valves are working, and the condition of the membrane surrounding the heart. Mitral valve prolapse, a common minor abnormality, often shows up on this test, as well as more serious problems.

Stress Test

Your heart rate, blood pressure, and EKG are constantly monitored as you exercise on a treadmill that goes faster and faster with a steeper and steeper incline. This test—also called an exercise tolerance test or treadmill test—should be performed in the presence of a cardiologist and in or near a hospital in case the strain causes heart problems that need emergency treatment. The test should be stopped immediately if you experience any light-headedness, chest pain, nausea, or palpitations.

What the results mean

The increasing strain on the heart causes changes that can tell your doctor if you are at risk of a heart attack. This is because a blockage in the coronary arteries—the blood vessels that feed your heart muscle—may show up only during exercise.

Angiography

A dye is injected into various arteries, and X rays are taken.

What the results mean

The doctor can detect blockages in the blood vessels that can lead to heart attack or stroke, as well as aneurysms (weakened spots in the blood-vessel walls). The test carries some risk of causing stroke.

✖ Kidney Tests

The two tests listed here involve taking X rays. Ultrasound (similar to an echocardiogram) can also be used to outline the kidneys.

Intravenous Pyelogram (IVP)

After an iodine-containing substance is injected into a vein, X rays are taken at five-minute intervals to show the outlines of the kidney, ureter, and bladder.

What the results mean

Tumors, kidney stones, and swelling of the kidney tissue can be seen, as well as blockage to urine flow or a mass that may be pressing on the kidney. A kidney that is not functioning will not appear on the X ray, and one in an abnormal position can be found.

Voiding Cystourethrogram (VCUG)

A technician will fill your bladder with a dye injected through a catheter and take X rays while you urinate.

What the results mean

If you have recurrent urinary-tract infections, the test will show if there is a significant backup of urine from the bladder into the ureter, in which case daily antibiotics may be needed to prevent infection. Investigating recurrent urinary tract infections is particularly important for children.

Magnetic Resonance Imaging (MRI)

MRI uses no radiation but produces pictures of the brain that are much more detailed than those of a CAT scan.

What the results mean

In addition to locating bleeding or tumors, as a CAT scan does, the test picks up subtle signs such as those of Parkinson's disease and multiple sclerosis in the brain or a herniated disc in the spinal column.

Mammography

- Only a small amount of radiation is used to take the mammogram. You usually stand up and put your breast on a photographic plate where it is compressed with a plastic shield or balloonlike device. It shouldn't hurt. If your breasts are tender at certain times in your menstrual cycle, schedule your mammogram when they are least sensitive.
- Mammograms can detect breast abnormalities at easily treated stages before you can feel them, but they are not foolproof. Examine your breasts monthly.

What the results mean

Mammograms can detect cysts, abscesses, and tumors. Whether a mass is benign or malignant is hard to tell in the early stages, so abnormalities usually need to be biopsied or removed totally to determine treatment.

How often to be tested

Although there is controversy over the benefits of mammography for women under 50, many experts still recommend having a first mammogram between ages 35 and 40, followed by one every two years between 40 and 50, and yearly thereafter. If your mother or sister has had breast cancer, consult your doctor for an appropriate schedule. And if you have a lump, pain, or nipple discharge, have a mammogram right away, no matter what your age.

You also should have a breast examination by a doctor at least every three years between ages 20 and 40, and every year after 40.

Pap Smear

- A routine part of every gynecological examination.
- Your doctor takes a painless swab from the cervix and vaginal walls and sends it to a lab for analysis.

What the results mean

Pap smears can detect not only cervical cancer but also inflammation and many infections, minor and more serious; they also provide important information about the state of your female hormones. A normal test is termed class I, and abnormal results are graded by degree into four classifications, with only the most severe—a class V test—signifying outright cancer. Treatment depends on the diagnosis and may range from doing nothing for a minor inflammation to, in rare cases, a hysterectomy for cancer. Because the error rate of Pap smears is high, the doctor should always repeat an abnormal test.

How often to be tested

Women who are on birth control pills and are sexually active should have a Pap smear every six months; other women should be checked every year.

Physical Examination

The routine physical exam generally includes a pulse and blood-pressure reading, measure of height and weight, blood tests (including a lipoprotein profile), fundoscopy, and sometimes other tests as well, such as a fecal occult blood test.

What the results mean

A physical exam serves as a general measure of health and sometimes picks up early signs of disease.

How often to have a physical exam

Most doctors no longer recommend yearly physicals for everybody. A good schedule to follow instead is to have a complete checkup every four or five years under age 40, every three years between 40 and 50, every two years between 50 and 60, and every year after that. At any age, you should have more frequent examinations if you have chronic medical problems such as diabetes or high blood pressure, are obese, or smoke cigarettes.

✖ Pulse

To take your own pulse, press two fingertips over the artery in your wrist, just below the base of the thumb. Count the beats in 20 seconds, then multiply by 3.

What the results mean

The normal pulse rate—the speed at which your heart pumps blood—is 60–80 beats a minute; it should be regular, without skipped or extra beats. Abnormal rates can be due to thyroid problems (too high causes a fast rate, too low a slow one), heart problems, anxiety (even the stress of a physical exam), or weakness from an illness such as the flu or other problems.

The character of your pulse is also important. A discrepancy between the strength of the pulse on one side of the neck and the other may mean you are in danger of a stroke. A pulse that is abnormally strong and bounding can signal a problem with a heart valve. If the pulse is weak, you may have blockages in your blood vessels from diabetes, atherosclerosis (hardening of the arteries), or a variety of other disorders.

✖ Stomach and Intestinal Tests

Though most of these tests are uncomfortable, they generally are not painful.

Barium Enema

Barium, a radioactive material, is instilled in your large intestine through a tube inserted into your anus. Because barium is constipating, drink fluids afterward. Don't be alarmed if you have white stools for a day or two.

What the results mean

The doctor will be able to see tumors or polyps, any obstructions, and other abnormalities.

Colonoscopy and Sigmoidoscopy

In colonoscopy, for which you will be sedated, the doctor looks into the colon with a flexible tube inserted into your anus. The procedure is essentially the same for sigmoidoscopy, except that the doctor looks only into the lower third of the intestine.

What the results mean

Your doctor can see where bleeding comes from, remove a polyp, or biopsy a mass.

Upper GI Series

You will be asked to down a drink of barium so that X rays can be taken of the esophagus, stomach, duodenum, and sometimes the small intestine.

What the results mean

Your doctor can diagnose swallowing disorders, hiatus hernias, ulcers, tumors, and some inflammations of the stomach and small bowel.

Fecal Occult Blood Test (FOBT)

A small sample of stool that remains on the doctor's glove after a rectal exam or that is collected by you at home is tested for blood that is invisible to the eye.

What the results mean

This test is done routinely as part of a regular checkup to detect the earliest sign of cancer of the colon. It is also part of an investigation of anemia or abdominal pain. If your test is positive, tell your doctor if you recently ate radishes, turnips, or red meat, took large doses of vitamin C or iron pills, or had a nosebleed. All of these things can produce misleading results.

Urinalysis

Urine can tell about the health not only of the kidneys but also of other organ systems.

What the results mean

Specific gravity is the degree to which your urine is concentrated or diluted. If it is persistently too dilute, your doctor may ask for a first morning sample to see how well your kidneys concentrate your urine overnight. Urine that is too concentrated may indicate poor fluid intake, decreased kidney function, or dehydration from vomiting and diarrhea.

Acidity or alkalinity (pH) is useful information when there is a history or possibility of kidney stones, urinary tract infection, or kidney disease.

Glucose or sugar in the urine may mean you have diabetes. You will need a blood test to confirm the diagnosis, as some families filter sugar easily through their kidneys but do not have any disease. Inflammation of the pancreas and thyroid problems also may cause sugar in the urine.

Blood in the urine may mean infection, a stone, or an inflammation of the kidney. Excessive exertion such as running sometimes causes some blood to leak into the urine; this usually disappears after resting.

Protein molecules are large and under normal conditions should not filter into the urine. However, they may appear in small amounts in the urine after strenuous exercise or an illness, especially one with a fever. In large amounts, protein in the urine warrants a search for an underlying kidney problem.

Nitrites, substances produced when bacteria multiply, may be the earliest or only sign of an infection.

White blood cells may be present because of a urinary tract or vaginal infection.

✖ X Ray

The simple X ray is a nonspecific test that is being replaced more and more by CAT scans, magnetic resonance imaging, and other tests.

What the results mean

An X ray can detect such things as an enlarged heart, a broken bone, a sinus infection, or pneumonia.

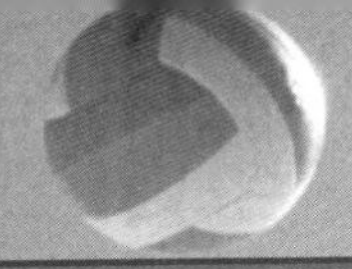

COUNTING YOUR CALORIES AND FAT GRAMS

Total calorie values for each item in this table were rounded to the nearest 5 calories (calories from fat and fat grams were not). The portion sizes are given in common household units and in grams. The portion size shown may not be the amount that you eat. If you choose larger or smaller portions than listed, increase or decrease the calorie and fat counts accordingly. Check nutrition labels on foods for additional information, including saturated fat, choles-terol, and sodium content.

Breads, Cereals, and Other Grain Products

Breads	Calories	Fat grams	Calories from fat
Bagel			
plain, 1, 3½" diam.	195	1	10
oat bran, 1, 3½"	180	1	8
poppy seed, 1, Sara Lee	190	1	9
Cracked-wheat bread, 1, 25 g slice	65	1	9
French bread, 1, 25 g slice	70	1	7
Pita bread			
white, 1, 6½" diam.	165		6
whole wheat, 1, 6½" diam.	170		15
Pumpernickel, 1, 32 g slice	80	1	9
Raisin, 1, 26 g slice	70	1	10
Rye, 1, 32 g slice	85	1	10
White			
regular, 1, 25 g slice	65	1	8
Wonder bread light, 2 slices, 45 g	80	1	9
Whole wheat			
regular, 1, 25 g slice	70	1	11
Wonder bread, 2 slices, 45 g	80	<1	14
Rolls			
Croissant, prepared w/butter, 1, 57 g	230	12	108
Dinner, 1, 28 g	85	2	19
Frankfurter or hamburger, 1, 43 g	125	2	20
French, 1, 38 g	105	2	15
Hard, 1 3½", 57 g	165	2	22
Quick breads, Biscuits, Muffins, Breakfast Pastries			
Biscuit			
plain, 2½" diam., 60 g	210	10	88
from dry mix, 3" diam., 57 g	190	7	62
from refrig. dough, 2½" diam., 27 g	95	4	36
Banana bread, 1 slice, 60 g	195	57	
Coffee cake			
cinnamon w/crumb topping, 63 g	265	15	132
butter streusel, Sara Lee, 41 g	160	7	63
Danish			
cheese, Sara Lee, individual, 36 g	130	8	72

	Calories	Fat grams	Calories from fat
cheese-filled, Entenmann's, fat-free 54 g	130	0	0
Doughnuts			
plain cake, 1, 47 g	200	11	97
glazed, 1, 45 g	190	10	93
English muffin, plain, 1, 57 g	135	1	9
Muffin			
blueberry, 1, 2½", 57 g	160	4	33
bran w/raisins, Dunkin' Donuts 1, 104 g	310	9	81
Pancake			
plain, from dry mix, 1, 56 g	200	1	9
plain, frozen Aunt Jemima, 3, 114 g	185	2	22
Waffle			
plain, 7" diam., 75 g	220	11	95
blueberry, frozen, Eggo, 2, 78 g	220	8	72
Breakfast Cereal			
All-Bran, ½ cup, 30 g	80	1	9
Bran flakes, ¾ cup, 28 g	100	1	9
Cheerios, 1¼ cup, 28 g	110	2	18
Corn flakes, 1 cup, 30 g	110	0	0
Cream of Wheat			
regular or instant, cooked, ⅔ cup, 168 g	100	0	0
instant, cooked, ⅔ cup, 161 g	100	<1	0
mix'n eat, 1 pkg., 28 g	100	0	0
Frosted Flakes, ¾ cup, 30 g	120	0	0
Frosted Mini-Wheats, 1 cup, 55 g	190	1	9
Grape-Nut Flakes, 1 cup, 28 g	100	1	9
Granola, date nut, Erewhon, ¼ cup, 28 g	130	6	50
Oatmeal			
reg., quick, or instant, cooked, 1 cup, 234 g	145	2	21
cinnamon & spice, instant , 1 pkg., 46 g	170	2	18
Raisin bran, 1 cup, 55 g	170	1	9
Rice Chex, 1 cup, 31 g	120	0	0
Rice Krispies, 1¼ cup, 30 g	110	0	0
Shredded wheat, Quaker	220	2	14
Special K, 1 cup, 30 g	110	0	0
Total, 1 cup, 28 g	100	1	9
Wheaties, 1 cup, 28 g	100	1	9
Pasta and Rice			
Macaroni			
cooked, plain, ½ cup, 65 g	95	<1	3
spinach, cooked, Ronzoni, ½ cup, 67 g	105	<1	4
Pasta			
fresh, cooked, plain, 1 cup, 170 g	225	2	16
homemade w/egg, cooked, 1 cup, ¡70 g	220	3	27
Ravioli, cheese, cooked, Contadina,			
⅓ container, 190 g	270	11	99
Rice, cooked, 1/2 cup			
Brown, medium grain, 98 g	110	1	7
White, glutinous, 120 g	115	<1	2
White, long grain instant, 82 g	80	<1	1

	Cal	Fat	
White, medium grain, 93 g	120	<1	2
Wild rice, 82 g	85	<1	3
Spaghetti, cooked, plain, 1 cup, 140 g	155	<1	4

Crackers

Cheez-it, Sunshine, 24 crackers, 32 g	140	8	72
Finn-Crisp dark, 3 crackers, 15 g	60	0	0
Matzo, plain, 1, 28 g	110	<1	4
Ritz, Nabisco, 4 crackers, 14 g	70	4	36
Saltine, 10 crackers, 28 g	120	4	36
Soup or oyster, 4 crackers, 14 g	70	4	36
Triscuit, Nabisco, 6 crackers, 28 g	120	4	36

Fruits

Fruits

(calories in cooked and canned fruit include both fruit and liquid)

Apple, raw, sliced, ½ cup, 55 g	30	<1	2
Applesauce, ½ cup			
sweetened, 128 g	95	<1	2
unsweetened, 122 g	50	<1	1
Apricots			
canned, heavy syrup, 3 halves, 85 g	70	<1	1
canned, light syrup pack, 3 halves, 85 g	55	<1	0
dried, cooked without sugar, ½ cup, 125 g	105	<1	2
raw, 4 halves, 78 g	35	<1	3
Avocados			
California, 3", ½, 86 g	155	15	135
Florida, 3⅝", ½, 152 g	170	13	121
Banana, medium, 114 g	105	1	5
Blueberries, ½ cup			
frozen, unsweetened, 78 g	40	<1	4
frozen, sweetened, 115 g	95	1	5
raw, 72 g	40	<1	3
Cherries, ½ cup			
raw, sweet, 72 g	50	1	6
sweet, frozen, sweetened, 130 g	115	<1	2
sour red, frozen, unsweetened, 78 g	35	<1	3
Cranberry sauce, sweetened, ¼ cup, 70 g	110	0	0
Dates, dried, 10, 83 g	230	<1	3
Fruit cocktail, canned, ½ cup			
juice pack, 124 g	55	<1	0
heavy syrup, 128 g	95	<1	1
Grapefruit, raw, 3¾", ½, 118 g	40	<1	1
Melon, honeydew, cubed, ½ cup, 85 g	30	<1	1
Oranges, ½ cup			
mandarin, canned, light syrup, 122 g	80	0	0
raw, sections, 90 g	40	<1	1
Peaches			
canned, in juice, ½ cup, 77 g	55	0	0
canned, in light syrup, ½ cup, 77 g	70	<1	1
Pears			
canned, in light syrup, 1 half, 77 g	35	<1	1
dried, without added sugar, ½ cup, 128 g	165	<1	4
Pineapple			
canned, juice pack, ½ cup, 125 g	75	<1	1
raw, diced, ½ cup, 78 g	40	<1	3
Plums			
canned, juice pack, 3, 95 g	55	<1	0
raw, 2⅛" diam., 66 g	35	<1	4
Prunes			
dried, cooked, without sugar, ½ cup, 106 g	115	<1	2
dried, uncooked, 10, 84 g	200	<1	4
Raisins, seedless, ¼ cup, 41 g	125	<1	2
Raspberries, ½ cup			
frozen, unsweetened, 125 g	61	1	6
raw, 62 g	30	<1	3
Rhubarb, cooked, sweetened, ½ cup, 120 g	140	<1	1
Tangerines, sections, ½ cup, 98 g	45	<1	2
Watermelon, 10" x 1", 480 g	155	2	19

Juices

Apple juice or cider, 1 cup, 249 g	120	0	0
Apricot nectar, canned, ¾ cup, 188 g	105	<1	2
Cranberry juice cocktail, ¾ cup, 190 g	110	<1	2
Grape juice			
bottled, ¾ cup, 188 g	110	0	0
from frozen concentrate, ¾ cup, 188 g	96	<1	2
Lemonade, ¾ cup			
homemade, prepared w/sugar, 186 g	90	0	0
from frozen concentrate, 186 g	75	<1	0
Orange juice, ¾ cup			
fresh, 186 g	85	<1	3
from frozen concentrate, 187 g	85	<1	1
Pineapple juice, canned, ¾ cup, 188 g	105	<1	1
Prune juice, canned, ¾ cup, 192 g	135	<1	1
Snapple, 1 bottle			
Dixie Peach, 295 g	140	0	0
Lemonade, 240 g	110	0	0
Passion Supreme, 309 g	160	0	0
Pink Grapefruit Cocktail, 249 g	120	0	0
V-8 juice, canned, ¾ cup, 182 g	35	0	0

Vegetables

Alfalfa sprouts, raw, 1 cup, 33 g	10	<1	2
Artichoke, cooked, medium, 120 g	60	<1	2
Asparagus, ½ cup			
canned, drained, 120 g	25	1	7
cooked, drained, 90 g	20	<1	3
Bean sprouts, Mung, raw, ½ cup, 52 g	15	<1	1
Beet greens, cooked, drained, ½ cup, 72 g	20	<1	1
Beets, ½ cup			
canned, sliced, drained, 85 g	25	<1	1
cooked, sliced, drained, 85 g	35	<1	1
Broccoli, ½ cup			
frozen florets, cooked, 71 g	20	0	0
raw, chopped, 44 g	10	<1	1
Brussels sprouts, cooked, drained, ½ cup, 78 g	30	<1	4
Cabbage, ½ cup			
Chinese bok choy, shredded, raw, 35 g	5	<1	1
shredded, raw, 35 g	10	<1	1
shredded, cooked, drained, 75 g	15	<1	3
Carrots			
frozen, sliced, cooked, drained, ½ cup, 73 g	25	<1	1
raw, 7½" x 1⅛", 72 g	30	<1	1
Cauliflower, ½ cup			
frozen, cooked, drained, 90 g	15	<1	2
raw, 1" pieces, 50 g	10	<1	1
Celery, raw			
cooked, drained, ½ cup, 75 g	15	<1	1
raw, 7½ in x 1¼", 40 g	5	<1	1

Food			
Corn, cooked			
canned, yellow, cream style, ½ cup, 128 g	90	1	5
canned, solids & liquid, ½ cup, 128 g	80	1	5
frozen, white, cooked, drained, ½ cup, 82 g	65	<1	1
on the cob, drained, 1 ear, 140 g	85	1	9
Cucumber, raw, sliced, ½ cup, 52 g	10	<1	1
Eggplant			
cooked, drained, 1" pieces, ½ cup, 48 g	15	<1	1
in tomato sauce, 1 cup, 231 g	75	<1	3
Green beans, ½ cup			
canned, drained, 68 g	25	0	0
cooked, drained, 62 g	20	<1	2
frozen, French style 85 g	25	0	0
raw, snap, 55 g	15	<1	1
Kale, cooked, drained, ½ cup, 65 g	20	<1	2
Lettuce			
iceberg, ¼ of a 6" head, 135 g	20	<1	2
looseleaf, shredded, ½ cup, 28 g	5	<1	1
romaine, shredded, ½ cup, 28 g	5	<1	4
Lima beans, cooked, drained, ½ cup, 85 g	105	<1	2
Mushrooms			
canned, pieces, drained, ½ cup, 78 g	20	<1	2
raw, whole, 1, 18 g	5	<1	1
shiitake, cooked, ½ cup, 73 g	40	<1	1
Onions			
canned, solids & liquid, 1", 63 g	10	<1	1
raw, chopped, ½ cup, 80 g	30	<1	1
Peas, green, ½ cup			
frozen, cooked, drained, 80 g	60	<1	2
raw, 72 g	50	<1	3
Peppers, sweet, red or green, ½ cup			
cooked, drained, 68 g	20	<1	1
raw, 50 g	15	<1	1
Potatoes			
baked, w/skin, 4¾" x 2⅓", 156 g	220	<1	2
boiled, no skin, 2½ inch diameter, 135 g	115	<1	1
hash browns, Ore-Ida frozen, 1 patty, 85 g	70	<1	0
mashed, w/whole milk, ½ cup, 105 g	80	1	6
scalloped, frozen, Stouffer's, ½ pkg., 165 g	135	6	52
Tater Tots, frozen, Ore-Ida, 1¼ cup, 85 g	160	7	63
Spinach, ½ cup			
frozen, cooked, drained, 95 g	25	<1	2
raw, chopped, 28 g	5	<1	1
Squash, ½ cup			
summer, cooked, drained, 90 g	20	<1	3
winter, baked cubes, 102 g	40	1	6
Sweet potatoes			
baked in skin, 5" x 2", 114 g	115	<1	1
canned, mashed, 128 g	130	<1	2
Tomato sauce, canned, ½ cup, 112 g	35	<1	2
Tomatoes, ½ cup			
canned, stewed, 103 g	35	0	0
raw, chopped, 90 g	20	<1	3
Turnip greens, cooked, drained, ½ cup, 72 g	15	<1	2
Turnips, cooked, mashed, ½ cup, 115 g	20	<1	1

Meat, Poultry, Fish, and Alternates

(Serving sizes are cooked, edible parts.)

Beef

Food			
Beef liver, 3 oz., 85 g			
braised	135	4	37
pan-fried	185	7	61
Corned beef, canned, 1 oz., 28 g	70	4	38
Ground beef, broiled, medium, 3 oz., 85 g			
extra lean	220	14	125
ground chuck	230	16	141
regular	245	18	158
Roast beef, 3 oz., 85 g			
bottom round, lean & fat	160	6	56
eye of round, lean & fat	195	11	98
pot roast, lean & fat	280	20	182
rib, lean & fat	300	24	216
tip round, lean & fat	160	7	60
Sirloin, broiled, lean & fat, 3 oz., 85 g	165	6	55
Veal, loin, lean only, roasted, 3 oz., 85 g	150	6	53
Lamb			
Ground lamb, broiled, 3 oz., 85 g	240	17	150
Leg of lamb, lean & fat roasted, 3 oz., 85 g	250	18	158
Shoulder chop, lean & fat, braised, 3 oz., 85 g	295	20	185
Pork			
Bacon, thick, broiled, 1 slice, 10 g	55	4	40
Bacon, Canadian, grilled, 1 slice, 23 g	45	2	18
Ham			
center slice, 3 oz., 85 g	170	11	99
canned, lean, 3 oz., 85 g	100	4	35
canned, regular, 3 oz., 85 g	190	13	116
Pork chop, loin, broiled, 3 oz., 85 g	205	11	100
Pork loin ribs, braised, 3 oz., 85 g	250	18	165
Pork roast, center loin, 3 oz., 85 g	200	11	103
Pork roast, sirloin, 3 oz., 85 g	175	8	72
Pork shoulder, roasted, 3 oz., 85 g	245	20	180
Sausage and Luncheon Meats			
Bologna, 1 slice, 28 g			
beef & pork	90	8	72
turkey	55	4	40
Braunschweiger, 1 slice, 18 g	65	6	52
Chicken breast			
Oscar Mayer, roasted, 1 slice, 28 g	25	<1	3
Healthy Choice, roasted, 3 slices, 28 g	30	<1	4
Ham, boiled, 1 slice, 21 g	20	1	9
Salami			
beef, 1 slice, 23 g	60	5	43
turkey, 10% fat, 1 oz., 28 g	45	3	24
Sausage, summer, beef, 1 slice, 23 g	70	6	54
Turkey			
Oscar Mayer, roasted, 1 slice, 28 g	25	1	7
Oscar Mayer, fat-free, smoked, 4 slices, 52 g	40	<1	3
Poultry			
Chicken breast, ½ breast			
boneless, w/out skin, roasted, 86 g	140	3	28
boneless, w/skin, flour fried, 98 g	220	9	78
Chicken drumstick, 1			
w/out skin, roasted, 72 g	75	2	22
w/skin, roasted, 81 g	110	6	52
Chicken liver, simmered, ½ cup, 70 g	110	4	34
Chicken, thigh, 1			
w/out skin, roasted, 71 g	110	6	51
w/skin, roasted, 81 g	155	10	86
Turkey, ground, cooked, 1 patty, 82 g	195	11	97

72

Food	Cal	Fat	Fat Cal
Turkey, roasted			
dark meat w/out skin, diced, ½ cup, 64 g	120	5	42
dark meat w/skin, 3 oz., 85 g	190	10	88
light meat w/out skin diced, ½ cup, 64g	100	2	19
light meat w/skin, 3 oz., 85 g	170	7	64
Turkey liver, simmered, ½ cup, 70 g	120	4	38

Fish and Shellfish

Food	Cal	Fat	Fat Cal
Anchovies, canned in oil, drained, 5, 20 g	45	2	17
Clams, canned, drained, ½ cup, 80 g	120	2	14
Fish fillets			
breaded, frozen, 2, 99 g	280	19	171
breaded, Healthy Choice, 1, 99 g	160	5	45
Flounder, cooked, dry heat, 3 oz., 85 g	100	1	12
Halibut, cooked, dry heat, 3 oz., 85 g	120	2	22
Salmon 3 oz., 85 g			
Chinook, cooked, dry heat	195	11	102
Chum, cooked, dry heat	130	4	37
Coho, cooked, moist heat	155	6	57
Sardines, Atlantic, canned in oil, drained solids, 2, 24 g	50	3	25
Sea Bass, cooked, dry heat, 3 oz., 85 g	105	2	20
Shrimp, cooked			
breaded & fried, 4, 30 g	75	4	33
moist heat, large, 4 22 g	20	<1	2
Tuna, light, canned in water, ½ cup, 74 g	85	1	5

Eggs

Food	Cal	Fat	Fat Cal
Fried, whole, 1, 46 g	90	7	62
Hard-cooked, whole, 1, 50 g	80	5	48
Poached, 1 whole, , 50 g	75	5	45
Scrambled, w/marg. & whole milk, 1, 64 g	105	8	7
Soft-boiled, whole, 1, 50 g	80	6	50
Whites, raw, 1, 33 g	15	0	0

Beans and Peas

Food	Cal	Fat	Fat Cal
Baked beans, canned			
pork & beans, tomato sauce, ½ cup, 114 g	100	1	13
w/pork, molasses & sugar, ½ cup, 126 g	190	6	58
Black-eyed peas, ½ cup			
canned, solids & liquid, 120 g	90	1	6
cooked, drained, ½ cup, 82 g	80	<1	3
Chickpeas (garbanzos), canned, ½ cup, 120 g	145	1	12
Black beans, cooked, ½ cup, 86 g	115	<1	4
Kidney beans, cooked, ½ cup, 88 g	110	<1	4
Lima beans, cooked, drained, ½ cup, 85 g	105	<1	2
Navy beans, cooked, ½ cup, 91 g	130	1	5
Refried beans, canned, ½ cup, 126 g	135	1	12

Nuts and Seeds

Food	Cal	Fat	Fat Cal
Almonds, unblanched			
dried, 3 Tbs., 28 g	165	15	133
dry roasted, 3 Tbs., 26 g	150	13	119
Cashews, dry roasted, 3 Tbs., 28 g	165	13	118
Coconut, dried, sweetened, flaked, 2 Tbs., 9 g	45	3	27
Peanut butter, 2 Tbs., 32 g	190	14	126
Peanuts, roasted			
dry roasted, 3 Tbs., 28 g	165	14	125
honey roasted, 3 Tbs., 28 g	170	14	126
Pecans, dried, ½ cup, 28 g	190	19	173
Pine nuts, dried, 1 Tbs., 10 g	50	5	46
Pistachios, dry roasted, 3 Tbs., 28 g	170	15	135
Sesame seeds			
Tahini, raw kernels, 1 Tbs., 15 g	85	7	65
dried, kernels, 1 Tbs., 8 g	45	4	39
Sunflower seeds, dry roasted, 3 Tbs., 28 g	165	14	127
Walnuts, dried, ¼ cup, 28 g	180	18	158

Meat Substitutes

Food	Cal	Fat	Fat Cal
Burger, vegetarian			
Vege burger, Natural Touch, 1, 64 g	140	6	54
Veggie Sizzler, nonfat, Soy Boy, 1, 85 g	90	0	0
Hot dog, Not Dogs, 1, 43 g	105	5	45
Tofu			
fried, 2¾ x 1 x ½", 29 g	80	6	53
regular, ½ cup, 124 g	95	6	53

Dairy Products

Cheese

Food	Cal	Fat	Fat Cal
American, light, 1 slice, 28g	70	4	36
Blue, crumbled (not packed), ¼ cup, 34 g	120	10	87
Brie, 1 oz., 28 g	95	8	70
Cheddar			
1" cube, 17 g	70	6	51
light, 1 slice, 28 g	70	4	36
Colby, 10 oz., 28 g	110	9	79
Cottage cheese, ½ cup			
creamed, large curd, 113 g	115	5	46
dry curd, 73 g	60	<1	3
low-fat, 1% fat, 113 g	80	1	10
Cream cheese, 2 Tbs.			
light, Philadelphia brand, 28 g	60	5	45
regular, 30 g	105	10	94
whipped, Philadelphia brand, 28 g	100	10	90
Feta, 1 oz., 28 g	75	6	54
Mozzarella, 1 oz., 28 g			
regular	80	6	54
part skim	70	4	40
Parmesan, grated, 1 Tbs., 5 g	25	2	14
Swiss			
1" cube, 15 g	55	4	37
light, 1 slice, 28 g	70	3	27

Cream

Food	Cal	Fat	Fat Cal
Half & half, 1 Tbs., 15 g	20	2	16
Heavy, whipping, 1 Tbs., 15 g	50	6	48
Sour cream			
cultured, 2 Tbs., 24 g	50	5	45
light, 50% less fat, 2 Tbs., 30 g	40	2	22
Whipped cream, pressurized, 1 Tbs., 3 g	10	1	6

Imitation Cream Products

Food	Cal	Fat	Fat Cal
Coffee creamers			
nondairy, liquid, Coffee Rich, 1 Tbs., 14 g	25	1	13
nondairy, liquid, Int'l Delight, 1 Tbs., 15 g	45	2	14
Sour cream			
imitation, cultured, nondairy, 2 Tbs., 28 g	60	5	49
imitation, nonbutterfat, 2 Tbs., 24 g	45	4	36
powdered, Coffee-Mate, 1 tsp., 2 g	10	1	6
Whipped topping			
nondairy, pressurized, 2 Tbs., 9 g	25	2	19
nondairy, frozen, Cool Whip, 1 Tbs., 4 g	10	1	7

Milk

Buttermilk, 1% fat, 1 cup, 245 g	100	2	19
Chocolate milk, 1 cup, 250 g			
low-fat, 1% fat	160	2	22
whole	210	8	76
Condensed, sweetened, 2 Tbs., 38 g	125	3	30
Evaporated, canned, 2 Tbs., 32 g			
low-fat	30	1	5
skim	25	<1	1
whole	40	2	21
Low-fat, 1% fat, 1 cup, 244 g	100	3	23
Skim, 1 cup, 245 g	85	<1	4
Whole, 3.3% fat, 1 cup, 244 g	150	8	73

Yogurt

Fruit flavors, custard, Yoplait, 1 cont., 170 g	190	4	36
Fruit-on-the-bottom, low-fat, 1 cont., 226 g	230	3	27
Plain, 1 cont., 226 g			
low-fat	145	4	32
nonfat	125	<1	4

Soups

Canned Soups

(Canned, condensed soups are prepared with water, unless otherwise noted.)

Bean & ham, Healthy Choice, ½ can, 228 g	220	4	36
Beef broth, ready-to-serve, 1 cup, 240 g	15	1	5
Black bean, Healthy Valley, 1 cup, 240 g	110	0	0
Chicken broth, ready-to-serve, ½ can, 249 g	30	3	27
Chicken noodle, Campbell's, 1 cup, 226 g	60	2	18
Chicken rice, 1 cup, 241 g	60	2	17
Clam chowder, New England			
frozen, Stouffer's 1 cup, 227 g	180	9	81
prepared w/skim milk, 1 cup, 233 g	100	2	18
prepared w/water, Campbell's, 1 cup, 224 g	80	2	20
Cream of Chicken, 1 cup, 244 g	110	7	62
Cream of mushroom, 1 cup			
prepared w/water, 244 g	130	9	81
prepared w/whole milk, 248 g	205	14	122
Minestrone			
prepared w/water, 1 cup, 241 g	80	3	23
ready-to-serve, Hain, ½ can, 270 g	160	3	27
Tomato, 1 cup			
prepared w/water, 244 g	85	2	17
prepared w/whole milk, 248 g	160	6	54
Vegetable			
prepared w/water, 1 cup, 241 g	90	1	9
ready-to-serve, Pritikin, ½ can, 209 g	70	0	0

Dried or Dehydrated Soups

Black bean, Nile Spice, 1 container, 309 g	180	1	5
Chicken vegetable, 1 cup, 251 g	50	1	7
Cream of chicken, 1 cup, 261 g	105	5	48
Mushroom, 1 cup, 253 g	95	1	44
Onion, 1 pkg., 7 g	20	<1	4
Split pea, 1 cup, 271 g	135	2	14
Tomato, 1 cup, 265 g	105	2	22

Desserts, Snack Foods, and Candy

Cakes

Angel food, 1/12 of 10" tube, 50 g	130	<1	1
Boston Cream Pie, ⅙ of 20 oz., 92 g	230	8	70
Carrot cake, Sara Lee, snack size, 1, 52 g	180	7	63
Cheesecake, plain, ⅙ of 17 oz., 80 g	255	18	160
Cupcake, 1			
chocolate, Hostess, 46 g	170	5	45
yellow, w/icing, 36 g	130	4	34
Devil's food, w/icing, ⅙ of 9", 69 g	235	8	72
Fruitcake, 1 slice, 34 g	140	4	35
Pound cake, Sara Lee, 1/10 of cake, 30 g	130	7	63
Yellow cake, w/icing, ⅛ of 8 oz., 64 g	240	9	84

Cookies and Bars

Brownies, chocolate			
frozen, Weight-Watchers, 1, 36 g	100	3	27
from mix, 2" square, 33 g	140	7	59
Chocolate chip			
Chips Ahoy!, 3, 32 g	160	8	72
refrigerated, Pillsbury, 2, 31 g	140	7	59
Creme sandwich, Nabisco, 2, 28 g	140	6	54
Fig bar, 2, 31 g	110	2	21
Gingersnaps, Sunshine, 6, 28 g	120	4	36
Graham crackers, 4, 1½" squares, 28 g	120	2	18
Oatmeal raisin, Barbara's, 2, 38 g	160	7	63
Oreo, Nabisco, 2, 28 g	100	4	36
Shortbread, 1⅝" square, 4, 32 g	160	8	69
Vanilla wafers, Nabisco, 7, 28 g	120	4	36

Pies

Apple, ⅛ of 9" pie, 155 g	410	19	175
Blueberry, ⅛ of 9" pie, 147 g	360	17	157
Cherry, ⅛ of 9" pie, 180 g	485	22	198
Chocolate cream, ⅛ of 9" pie, 142 g	400	23	206
Custard, ⅛ of 9" pie, 127 g	260	11	102
Lemon meringue, ⅛ of 9" pie, 127 g	360	16	147
Pumpkin, ⅛ of 9" pie, 155 g	315	14	130

Other Desserts

Custard, baked, ½ cup, 141 g	150	7	60
Frozen yogurt, vanilla, ½ cup			
Häagen-Dazs, 98 g	160	2	22
Yoplait, soft, 72 g	90	3	27
Gelatin, Jell-O, ½ cup, 140 g	80	0	0
Ice cream, vanilla, ½ cup			
regular, 10% fat, 66 g	135	7	65
Häagen-Dazs, 106 g	260	17	153
Ice cream, chocolate, ½ cup			
regular, 10% fat, 66 g	145	7	65
Häagen-Dazs, 106 g	270	17	153
Ice milk sandwich, Weight Watchers, 78 g	160	4	36
Juice bars			
Strawberry, Fruit'n Juice, Dole, 74 g	70	0	0
Strawberry, Welch's, 85 g	80	0	0
Puddings, from mix, prepared w/2% milk			
butterscotch, ½ cup, 148 g	150	2	20
chocolate, ½ cup, 147 g	150	2	20
tapioca, ½ cup, 141 g	145	2	22

	Calories	Fat (g)	Fat Calories
vanilla, ½ cup, 144 g	140	2	20
Sherbet, ½ cup, 87 g	135	2	17

Snack Foods

	Calories	Fat (g)	Fat Calories
Corn chips, ¾ cup, 28 g	155	9	85
Crackers (see Crackers)			
Nuts (see Nuts and Seeds)			
Popcorn			
air-popped, 1 cup, 8 g	30	<1	3
microwave, natural flavor, 1 cup, 8 g	35	2	18
Potato chips, 1 cup, 28 g	150	10	90
Pretzels			
Dutch, twisted, 2¾", 2, 32 g	120	1	10
Sticks, 2½ x ⅛", 60, 30 g	115	1	9
Twists, thin, Rold Gold, 10, 28 g	110	1	9

Candy

	Calories	Fat (g)	Fat Calories
Caramel, plain, ¾ inch, 8 g	30	1	6
Fudge, chocolate, 1 cu inch, 17 g	65	1	13
Gum drops, 8, 28 g	110	0	0
Hard candy, 5, 28 g	105	0	0
Jellybeans, 10 large or 26 small, 28 g	105	<1	1
Hershey's Kisses, 6, 28 g	150	9	81
Lollipops, 1, 28 g	110	0	0

Beverages

(Milk and juices are in Dairy Products and Fruits sections.)

Carbonated Sodas

	Calories	Fat (g)	Fat Calories
Cola, 1½ cup, 370 g	150	<1	0
Diet cola, w/aspartame, 1½ cup, 355 g	4	0	0
Gingerale, 1½ cup, 366 g	125	0	0
Grape soda, 1½ cup, 372 g	160	0	0
Lemon-lime, 1½ cup, 368 g	145	0	0
Orange soda, 1½ cup, 372 g	180	0	0
Root beer, 1½ cup, 370 g	150	0	0

Coffee and Tea

	Calories	Fat (g)	Fat Calories
Coffee			
brewed, 1 cup, 235 g	5	<1	0
brewed, decaffeinated, 1 cup, 240 g	3	0	0
instant, 1 cup, 240 g	5	0	0
Tea, brewed, 1 cup 237 g	2	<1	0
Tea, brewed herb, unflavored, 1 cup, 236 g	2	<1	0
Tea, iced, instant, lemon flavored			
sweetened w/aspartame, 1 cup, 259 g	2	0	0
sweetened w/sugar, made w/4 tsp., 23 g	85	<1	0

Alcoholic Beverages

	Calories	Fat (g)	Fat Calories
Beer, 1½ cup, 355 g			
light	100	0	0
regular	145	0	0
nonalcoholic	50	0	0
Gin, Rum, Whiskey, or Vodka, 80 proof, 1 jigger, 42 g	95	0	0
Wine, 1 glass			
red, 147 g	105	0	0
white, 147 g	100	0	0
Wine cooler, 1 glass, 360 g	175	<1	0

	Calories	Fat (g)	Fat Calories
Wine, dessert, 1 glass			
dry, 59 g	75	0	0
sweet, 59 g	90	0	0

Fats, Oils, and Condiments

Fats and Oils

	Calories	Fat (g)	Fat Calories
Butter			
regular or unsalted, 1 tsp., 5 g	35	4	37
whipped, 1 Tbs., 11 g	80	9	80
Margarine			
spread, tub, 1 Tbs., 14 g	75	9	75
stick, 1 Tbs., 14 g	100	11	100
Oil			
corn, 1 Tbs., 14 g	120	14	122
olive, 1 Tbs., 14 g	120	14	122
vegetable spray, 1¼ seconds, 1 g	5	1	5
Salad dressing			
blue cheese, 1 Tbs., 15 g	75	8	72
French 1 Tbs., 16 g	65	6	57
French, low-calorie, 1 Tbs., 16 g	20	1	9
Italian, 1 Tbs., 15 g	70	7	64
Italian, low calorie, 1 Tbs., 16 g	15	1	12
mayonnaise-like, 1 Tbs., 15 g	55	5	43
thousand island, 1 Tbs., 16 g	60	6	50
Barbecue sauce, 1 Tbs., 15g	15	<1	3
Catsup, 1 Tbs., 15 g	15	<1	0
Gravy, canned			
au jus, ¼ cup, 60 g	10	<1	1
beef, ¼ cup, 58 g	30	1	12
chicken, ¼ cup, 60 g	45	3	30
turkey, ¼ cup, 60 g	30	1	11
Horseradish, prepared, 1 tsp., 5 g	2	<1	0
Mustard, prepared, 1 tsp., 5 g	4	<1	2
Olives			
black, canned, small, 3, 10 g	10	1	9
green, medium, 4, 13 g	15	2	14
green, stuffed, 10, 34 g	35	4	34
Pickles			
dill, kosher spears, 1, 28 g	5	0	0
sweet, gherkins, small, 2½", 2, 30 g	40	<1	0
Relish, sweet pickle, 2 Tbs., 30 g	40	<1	1
Soy sauce, tamari, 1 Tbs., 18 g	10	<1	0
Tartar sauce, 1 Tbs., 14 g	75	8	68

Sugar, Jams, and Jellies

	Calories	Fat (g)	Fat Calories
Chocolate syrup			
fudge-type, 2 Tbs., 42 g	145	6	51
thin-type, 2 Tbs., 38 g	82	<1	3
Honey, 1 Tbs., 21 g	65	0	0
Jams and preserves, 1 Tbs., 20 g	50	<1	0
Jellies, 1 Tbs., 19 g	50	<1	0
Maple syrup, 2 Tbs., 40 g	105	<1	1
Sugar			
brown, unpacked, 1 cup, 145 g	545	0	0
white, granulated, 1 tsp., 4 g	15	0	0

Fast Foods

Burgers and Sandwiches

Burger King

Big Fish	700	41	370
Broiler Chicken	550	29	260
Double Cheeseburger with Bacon	640	39	350
Hamburger	330	15	140
Whopper	640	39	350

McDonald's

Big Mac	530	28	250
Filet-O-Fish	360	16	150
Hamburger	270	10	90
McChicken	570	30	270
McGrilled Chicken	510	30	270

Wendy's

Big Bacon Classic	610	33	290
Chicken Club	500	23	200
Grilled Chicken Sandwich	310	8	70
Hamburger, with everything	420	20	180

Salads, Fries, and Miscellaneous

(Salad values are given for salads without dressing.)

Burger King

Broiled Chicken Salad	200	10	90
French fries, medium	370	20	180
Garden Salad	100	5	45
Salad dressing, 30 g, thousand island	140	12	110
Salad dressing, 30 g, ranch	180	19	170
Salad dressing, 30 g, reduced-calorie Italian	15	<1	5

McDonald's

Chef Salad	210	11	100
Fajita Chicken Salad	160	6	60
French fries, large	450	22	200
French fries, small	210	10	90
Salad dressing, 1 pkg., blue cheese	190	17	150
Salad dressing, 1 pkg., lite vinaigrette	50	2	20
Salad dressing, 1 pkg., ranch	180	19	170

Pizza Hut

Breadsticks, 5	770	25	223
Buffalo wings, 12	565	35	310
Cheese pizza, ⅛ of med., thin crust	205	8	75
Cheese pizza, ⅛ of med., pan pizza	260	11	98
Pepperoni pizza, ⅛ of med., thin crust	215	10	69
Veggie Lover's, ⅛ of med., thin crust	185	7	61

Wendy's

Baked potato, plain	310	0	0
Baked potato w/chili and cheese	620	24	220
Baked potato w/sour cream and chives	380	6	60
Deluxe Garden Salad	110	6	50
Salad dressing, 2 Tbs., blue cheese	170	19	170
Salad dressing, 2 Tbs., fat-free French	30	0	0
Salad dressing, 2 Tbs., ranch	90	10	90

Desserts

Burger King

Dutch apple pie	300	15	140

McDonald's

Baked apple pie	260	13	120
Cookies	260	9	80

Pizza Hut

Dessert pizza, ⅛ of med.	245	5	46

Wendy's

Chocolate chip cookies, 1, 57 g	270	11	100